Navigating into the Second Cognition

The Map for Your Journey into Higher Conscious Awareness

By

Endall Beall

First Edition

Dedication

This book is dedicated to those who have made
the journey this far.

Table of Contents

ACKNOWLEDGEMENTS

I want to thank all of my spiritual companions who have served as sounding boards to help me solidify much of the information contained in this volume. There is no need to name names, they all know who they are, and everyone of them has my profound gratitude for their contributions to this body of work.

Once again I wish to acknowledge Richard Redhawk for allowing me to use his phenomenal artwork for this cover.

FOREWORD

This book is the fourth installment of *The Evolution of Consciousness* series. The series is a progressive unfolding of information necessary to advance one's own cognitive awareness. If you have not read the first three installments of this series, you will probably find that reading this book will be similar to walking in on the middle of a movie. Certain terms and concepts were introduced in the previous works and those terms will be used freely in this book without recapping their meaning.

It is highly recommended that one digests the material in the previous volumes in order to have a fuller understanding of what is presented in this volume. This is not requested as a shallow means to generate book sales. The author is presenting a linear unveiling of information which, when read in sequence of release, portrays an overall picture of what the problem is and what one will most likely encounter on their own path to higher conscious awareness. The author has no intent to rehash books already written in order to boost sales revenues. There is already enough of that in the spiritual marketplace as it is.

The reader should view this entire series as information for an ongoing personal educational process, not simply a presentation of supposition or theoretical propositions. As with any course material in any institute of higher learning, these books follow a guideline for progressive learning.

These books are written for the serious-minded individual who has an unswerving desire to know spirit, and ultimately to know themselves. This body of work is not for the spiritual tourist, those who still chase fanciful notions in their spiritual pursuits, those who feel they already have the answers for their own chosen path to enlightenment, or for those who are into pop spiritualism as the latest social fad as some kind of group endeavor.

Introduction

This body of work is designed to answer many of the questions presented in the previous works. Where the preliminary three volumes discussed the overall problems associated with, and identification of the first cognition, this volume works to explain how to navigate oneself through the transitional process into the second cognition.

Moving into a higher state of self-awareness and cognitive awareness are the same thing, for it is in finding the real person that lays buried inside all of us that is the real quest for understanding spirit. The first part of the journey is in unraveling all the perceptions predicated on the superficial illusions of the first cognition. The problem has to be identified in order to understand exactly what we are seeking to find in ourselves. The first volumes of this series have gone to great lengths to identify the problem and offer the solution.

There is no cut and dried method on how to achieve the things that will be explained in this book, for the simple reason that everyone is different. In this book, the author shares some of his own personal experiences during his own transitional period, along with certain generalizations observed with others who have walked their own path beside the author. How each person deals with this information, how they adapt it in developing their own solutions, is where the importance lies in this presentation.

I want every reader to understand that you are ultimately in charge of progressing yourself, and don't fall into the mindset that there is any rigid set rules or procedures to follow as to how you navigate your own way through your own period of transition. The reason so many have failed on their spirit path to date is through buying into the idea that there is one hard-coded set of rules that everyone must abide by in order to succeed. There are no such rules beyond overcoming one's own ego.

What is most needed in order for people to progress is valid information, not speculation. Unfortunately, for thousands of years humanity has followed the speculators about spirit rather than those who actually knew the difference. These speculators have been the foundation for spiritual misunderstanding throughout the ages, and it is due to their wild speculations that so few have managed to progress into the second cognition - i.e. find enlightenment.

The purpose of these books is to provide the reader with the tools of comprehension to finally start to understand why they have not progressed in advancing their spirit selves. The author was no different than the reader in the respect that there is so little truly usable information in the spiritual marketplace. These books are to designed to alleviate that dearth of information and give the reader something they can finally get their teeth into where understanding their own conscious advancement is concerned.

What is presented here is not just the *opinion* of the author. There is no shortage of opinions and speculations in the spiritual marketplace as it is, and if one wants speculation and mystical opinions about spirit, then it is suggested that one reads other works that abound in the marketplace written by opinionated spiritual speculators.

Chapter 1

"They do not understand me; I am not the mouth for these ears."

Friedrich Nietzsche - Thus Spake Zarathustra

There are many readers who have started reading this body of work for the simple reason that they have searched and searched for answers, trying to quench an internal thirst for understanding. Many have read multitudes of books on spirit, religion and esoteric studies trying to find an answer for this internal quest. Many readers find themselves at a standstill because they have exhausted most of the material in the marketplace and have become almost resigned to being stuck in the predicament of knowing there is more, on an instinctual gut level, yet not being able to find any source of information that provides any real answers or direction for what they are seeking.

The spiritual arena is rife with speculators printing numerous books on what they *think* spirit is, or at least what spirit *should be* from their own limited seats of perception. In virtually all these cases, they are making suppositions, usually founded on ancient traditions of mysticism or esotericism, which in turn were founded on the same faulty system of incorrect assumptions and suppositions. This system is the first cognition.

As the Nietzsche quote at the chapter head indicates, those operating in the first cognition only seek to have their perceptual world validated. They only want to hear what the first cognition demands reality to be. Spiritual undertakings are no exception to this rule of perceptual validation. One adopts the idea that spiritual studies or spiritual advancement is expected to be mystical, so people firmly rooted in the first cognition embrace that perceptual illusion and refuse to relinquish such notions. When someone like this author comes along to tell the no-nonsense truth about spirit, they refuse to hear the words because it goes against their own *beliefs* about what they think spirit *should* be. In that regard, this truth is not for their ears.

To help you understand this process in an allegorical fashion, I am going to use the analogy of an hourglass. When we are all fully engaged in the perceptions of the first cognition, our consciousness is filled to capacity with those perceptions, represented by the top of the hourglass. As we move to erode those perceptual illusions, the control of the first cognition gradually starts to diminish as we near the center of the hourglass, that narrow bottleneck through which the sand passes.

Many people reach that bottleneck in the hourglass and feel they have reached enlightenment. A good example of such people can be found in the Buddhist religion. Buddhism's greatest claim to fame is removing the ego. Many Buddhist teachers have succeeded in that aspect of transitioning into the second cognition, but they have become stuck at the bottleneck of the hourglass and have not progressed beyond it to grow in the second cognition.

The bottleneck of the hourglass can be allegorically viewed as a doorway into the second cognition. One can reach the threshold without passing through to the other side. Another way to view this being stuck in the bottleneck of the hourglass could be portrayed with the idea that someone is flying to another part of the world. The plane lands, but they do not disembark, yet they still make the claim that they have visited the country in which the plane landed. In the case with the Buddhist spiritual mentality, they have reached the doorway at the bottleneck of the hourglass, but they have not disembarked to really discover the new country that awaits them deeper into the second cognition. In essence their spiritual plane has landed, but they have chosen to stay on board rather than explore or become familiar with the new territory of the second cognition.

This being stalled is a result of not only perceiving enlightenment as a destination, but that the destination only entails beating the ego. Setting the ego aside in and of itself does not take one off the plane into the new country. To see where Buddhist mentality is still bound in this regard, we only have to look at how the monks maintain their first cognition ego habits. They adopt the dress of the institution, and still cater to being compassionate to other human beings as the justification for their religious perceptions. They profess the superiority of their belief system over other belief systems, and as such, they are still as firmly rooted in the first cognition as they were before they started on their quest for enlightenment. They are all still coloring within the perceptual lines of the first cognition.

In a sort of tragic sense, although they have set aside certain trappings of the ego, their ego habits still rule them, and they are exhibiting a state of egoless ego. I know the term seems to be an oxymoron, but I explained in *Demystifying the Mystical* how the ego is the ultimate deceiver. In the case of Buddhism, the ego personality has given in to the desires for the quest to enlightenment, but because they maintain the trappings, belief and proselytizing of their religion, their ego has simply changed shaped to suit the desires of the ego. It presents itself as being egoless, but it still follows the rules of any other first cognition ego - thus my observation about it being egoless ego. They are all still on the plane of the first cognition.

Throughout our lives we have all been indoctrinated and have learned to emulate the first cognition. This emulating, predicated on programming, is what keeps the system as a self-sustaining trap for consciousness. The first cognition is a closed loop for all those functioning within it. There is no escape from it using the tools and definitions of that locked-in system, and this is why one has to resort to allegory, analogy and metaphor to try and describe the second cognition. There is presently no vocabulary in the first cognition to describe the second cognition.

It is only through time and retrospection that we can see how seemingly innocuous circumstances in our lives have served as sort of an unwitting springboard on our path to understanding the second cognition. As a youth, I discovered and read my first science fiction novel when I was 13 years old. After that first novel, I developed a taste for science fiction and fantasy. This seemingly innocuous circumstance, in retrospect, served as a catalyst to inflame my imagination. Reading such material provided me the intellectual impetus to ask, "what if such things were possible?" It is this same sense of imagination that drove me on my own spirit quest later in life.

It was only late in life that I even tripped to embarking on my own spirit path. It was not an area of interest to me until I happened across the first book that sparked the drive in me to know more. Once that flame was lit, I couldn't digest material fast enough as I sought to discover whatever this mysterious thing called spirit was. The keener the inner desire to know got, the wider I broadened my areas of study, from new age material into layman's quantum theories and comparative religions.

Like most of the readers, I had no concept of what I was seeking, but was lured by the mental imaginings of becoming some kind of supernaturally gifted individual, with ideas of maybe healing the sick, or saving mankind from itself in some regard by being some kind of spiritual master. However, over time and tireless years of research, I became more and more disenchanted with these ideas. I found that no matter how the spiritual teachings were presented, no matter what doctrine or dogma they were wrapped in, they all lacked providing any solid solutions.

It was this personal disgust with the so-called teachers of these concepts that drove me onward to discover what it was that no one else could explain, except through spiritual speculations and opinion. The more I looked, the more I saw the repeating pattern in the information. Certain authors approached these concepts in different manners, but in the end, they call came up with the mystical illusion of spirit as the solution, and they all left me wanting.

Internally, I knew there was more, only I could not discover anyone who claimed to be an authority that could provide any kind of explanation about what that was. The harder I pushed to winnow through the mind-aching riddles of spiritual teachings, it seemed the more elusive it became. I can think of few things more frustrating than having an internal knowing about something and not being able to find anything that satisfies that internal gnawing for understanding. Many people encounter this frustration and just plain give up because they become resigned to the idea that maybe there just isn't anything more to this spirit stuff than wishful thinking, and they give it all up. Many abandon their quest over this sense of discouragement.

If you are reading these words, you have not given up that quest. You are still seeking answers; many of you after you have come to the realization that there is hardly a thing out there to feed your inner knowing. You have hoped against hope to one day find something, anything, that will provide some guidance and explanations about what you are experiencing. It is the desire of this author that you feel you have found that source of information.

Chapter 2

"And let everything break that can be broken by our truths! Many a house is still to be built!"

Friedrich Nietzsche - Thus Spake Zarathustra

If you have been strong enough to digest the first three volumes of this series, then you should have come away with an altering perception of the world in which we live. You should understand what is meant by a perceptual illusion hiding behind the mask of accepted beliefs. If you have worked with the processes described in *Demystifying the Mystical*, some of you may have encountered and defeated your own internal ego program, and you have embarked in working with energies and understanding them better.

As one moves on this path, if they don't get stuck in doctrinal nonsense and faulty beliefs, they find themselves doubting things a lot. This system of perpetual doubt on things you don't yet understand can be a catalyst to launch you further, provided you don't let such doubts paralyze you into inaction.

As you work your way down to the bottleneck of the hourglass, as you erode your own perceptual ego illusions, you will most likely be confronted with doubt about whether what you are seeking is attainable, or whether it is worth the effort to pursue it. This is especially true when you begin to get that sense of isolation from those around you. If you reach the level of eroding many of your former beliefs, you find yourself uncomfortable as you are moving away from the first cognition. You fear losing friends or family, and for too many people, this fear prevents them from moving forward.

As I progressed on my path I set the intent that all those who would serve as an impediment to my own personal development fade out of my life. I did not have to confront anyone in the sense of telling them to take a hike, but my stated intent created a program of intent around me where those who would be detrimental to my development simply moved on and found other people with which to associate. Naturally, I also had to accept the responsibility for what I was doing, so the loss of the few fair-weather friends I had was a price I was willing to pay in order to advance myself.

I said in all the previous works that your path is a personal one. It is nice to have the support of another who is on the same path to personal advancement as you are, but that is not always what happens. You have to be selfishly self-oriented to succeed in this endeavor. The reason I feel I advanced the way I did is because I would let nothing and no one stand in the way of my personal advancement. I was willing to pay any price, no matter how high it seemed, in order to advance my consciousness. Don Juan described this internal drive as *unbending intent.*

Many people find themselves too weak to extract themselves from the first cognition. They want to keep their friends and their social circles. They want to continue to live their lives in the first cognition without having to pay the price to advance themselves. This is why I have stated repeatedly to ask yourself whether you are ready to pay all costs necessary to advance your awareness. The speed of your advancement is going to depend on what you are willing to sacrifice in order to find what you are seeking.

Understand, there is no deadline to this process, and one can move as fast as they are willing to put forth effort into succeeding. It is a time consuming process whether you push yourself as hard as you can or not, but it will take substantially longer if one chooses to dawdle along the way. The more one farts around with the process, the longer it is going to take, provided one maintains the kind of focus required to succeed. Without that focus and dedication, even in a part time manner, you may as well give up now.

The meaning of the heading quote can be found in understanding destroying your own illusions - "breaking everything than can be broken". I explained about cognitive dissonance in the previous books. From the standpoint of psychology, most people do everything they can to avoid cognitive dissonance. Those in the first cognition are completely satisfied to maintain their own beliefs rather than face uncomfortable truths. From the standpoint of a first cognition psychologist, one on the spirit path would have to be crazy to intentionally seek bouts of cognitive dissonance. Unfortunately, cognitive dissonance comes with the territory of personal advancement. When I tell you that you have to read things with which you currently disagree, it means that in reading such things your own personal perceptual barriers will start to whittle away.

In the Western societies, Communism is the opposing doctrine to Capitalism. I was raised in the U.S. and had plenty of anti-Communist dogma shoved down my throat, culturally speaking. I never had an interest in Communism, and still don't insofar as embracing it as a viable political option. But late in life I read Marx's *Communist Manifesto* in order to see what it was all about. You can maybe understand my utter dismay to discover that the 10 Planks of the *Communist Manifesto* have been already put in place in the U.S.! This realization created a sense of cognitive dissonance within me. Here I had spent my entire life expressing hatred of Communism and all it stood for, only to find out that the nation I lived in had adopted all the principles of the doctrine I hated.

The Communist Party of American ran a candidate in presidential elections for years. Then one year they stopped putting up a candidate for election. When the person was asked why he chose to not run any more, he simply stated that the U.S. government had adopted and implemented all of Marx's tenets, so there was no point in running any more.

What I just showed is how my own perceptions were shaken through discovering a horrible truth. This is only one of many that happened to me over the years of my own whittling away of my own perceptual belief system. Don Juan once expressed to Castenada that one will not advance into the second cognition by only reading what they agree with. It takes facing what we disagree with that brings us these revelations of truth that destroy the perceptual illusions of our own beliefs.

When I discovered this truth about Communism, I could have denied it and refused to believe it. Many react to truth by denying it. Denying such truths does not make them go away, it only means that you are avoiding admitting the truth that you have discovered because it makes your ego psychologically uncomfortable. Denial will not take you to the second cognition.

What I used as my own bellwether in doing alternative research is when I found someone telling me that I shouldn't read or believe something. That is the first place I would go investigating. My own drive to know made me question why anyone wouldn't want me to look into a different account than their belief, or see an alternative perspective. Where many people would simply agree with the messenger and not investigate any further, the prompt to not go there is what made me look. For years I was told to not read Nietzsche because Hitler had used his writings as a foundation for the Nazi Party and the idea of the Aryan Master Race. When I read a few of Nietzsche's works for the first time, before moving into the second cognition and fully understanding his work, I saw even then that there was no way Nietzsche would ever support the likes of Hitler. Through his writings he expressed an extreme distaste for the Aryans, defining the root of the word, 'arya', to translate into meaning 'the owners'.

I am not saying that everything you look into as an alternative is true. What I *am* saying is that if you don't investigate it on your own, you will never know the difference. We live in an information age. The creation and development of the internet has become a powerful tool, both as an accessible platform for information, but equally so for disinformation. At the beginning of our journey into spirit, it is hard for us to tell the truth from the lies, the information from the disinformation.

As you progress on your personal journey, you will be confronted with many viewpoints in matters of spirit. You can find tons of videos on Youtube, which can be manufactured by anyone to paint the picture they want you to see. This is particularly true with purported spiritual material, and the vast majority of what is out there is simply wrong.

If you have been on this path very long, you have probably looked into esoteric traditions like the Kabala, the traditions of Aliester Crowley, the Rosicrucian's or the Freemasons. You may be one of those who has had a passing interest in the UFO aspects of spirituality, or you may have looked into the messages from a multitude of channelers in your search for understanding. You may have digested videos about how to alter your DNA or do what is called Quantum Jumping, astral projections, investigated 528hz frequencies and other frequencies supposedly designed to speed up your spiritual advancement. You may have even moved into studying Reiki practices or become a Reiki practitioner, thinking you are doing something spiritual in the process.

If you have done any of these things, chances are that you are still as spiritually lost as you were when you started. The reason for this is that all of these things rely on something external as a solution to your inner quest. No external form of exercise or ritual will move you an inch closer because your quest for understanding lies within yourself. This is why the followers of all these varied traditions are still mostly stuck in the mud where their own personal advancement is concerned.

About the same time I discovered my first spiritual book, I also discovered the conspiratorial version of history - what is referred to as 'Revisionist History". These days, in some circles, both of these subjects are so intimately intertwined as to be inseparable. There are popular shock jocks and spiritual writers who make their bread and butter selling gloom and doom scenarios in order to peddle their own brand of pap. This is not to say that there are not now, or have been in the past, those who have an agenda for world domination in one guise or another, but the sad truth is that what sells as conspiracy theory is designed to evoke emotional reactions - usually fear - in its believers.

After I discovered the conspiracy aspect of history, I eventually read a couple of pieces that pointed to certain laws enacted in the U.S. that proved the writer's assertions. Not being willing to simply take their word for it, I made my way into a law library to check out the writer's claims. This first venture into reading the law has led to a more eye-opening aspect of my development than I could ever foresee.

Where history is concerned, people can write and say virtually anything they want, so long as there are just enough facts to support their contentions or opinions. History has been written and rewritten many times over the ages, and at best, it is a questionable source of information. The basic truth is that people lie. There is a lot of viable and valuable research by the 'revisionists', and it makes the controllers of our perception very nervous, especially when revisionist history uncovers the lies of the status quo.

Many people embrace the conspiratorial view of history by simply listening to the doomsday shock jocks, or reading alleged historical accountings put out by the panic mongers, who are just as interested in selling books as any new age guru or spiritual teacher. One can question the conspiratorial view of history, and whether it is actually real or not, but when one finds specific incidents of this ongoing subversion of nations written into the laws, it is no longer conspiracy fiction but conspiracy fact. This is what my own path to discovery revealed to me. You can't deny what is enacted into law. The law says what it says, and when you find such evidence embedded in the laws of nations, conspiracy is no longer theoretical.

I am not going to delve into who these conspirators are at this point as it goes beyond the scope of this presentation. I am only bringing it up to share just another step on my own road to discovery and how certain perceptual illusions unraveled for me. I am telling these stories to prompt the reader to not accept anything that you think you know or don't know at face value. Only deeper inquiry will lead one to answers. Each of you has questions and doubts. That is a normal part of this process, but let doubt serve as the catalyst to make you dig deeper rather than leaving you simply wondering. Had I not ventured into studying the law, I would not have made the discoveries I did for myself. Had I not read that one article that piqued my curiosity to investigate more deeply into the law, I would not have discovered what I did that enhanced my own understanding and ultimately destroyed another set of my own perceptual illusions.

As you move along your path, you have to become attuned to certain signals, or tweaks you get in regard to researching something further. Most people disregard these tweaks and therefore discover nothing. When you set your unbending intent on succeeding on your quest into the second cognition, certain aspects of a larger consciousness will put things in your path in order to see if you are developing the intuitive sensitivity to pick up on such innocuous seeming clues. Your intuitive senses have to develop and become keener in order to pick up on these clues. You have to learn to read beyond the superficial in order to see the man behind the curtain manipulating the pictures of the first cognition. Believe nothing as it seems, yet remain open to possibilities as your intuitive skills develop.

Chapter 3

"To one person loneliness is the flight of the sick;
to another it is flight *from* the sick."

Friedrich Nietzsche - Thus Spake Zarathustra

On the beginning of our paths, we most often seek other like-minded individuals who can help to reinforce our belief systems about spiritual pursuits. We have an inner desire to find someone who may serve as a more informed guide that can possibly help us in our quest. Although I was not personally prey to many of the affectations of the *social spiritualist*, I managed to avoid a lot of the trappings of being involved with the procedures of group practices. In all honesty, I found many such practices pretty shallow and lacked genuineness. Using the Hindu pressing together of hands and saying *Namaste* seemed utterly pretentious to me, and it still does. All the happy, giddy faces and the huggy-kissy group endorsement appeared to be to be just as extremely shallow and superficial, and to be totally honest, such practices always looked and felt goofy to me. I guess you could say I always had a center of pragmatism when it came to my own spiritual development. Spiritual understanding has always been a serious endeavor to me, not a flight of fancy.

You are going to have to develop the same sort of pragmatic, serious approach for yourself if you intend to succeed. You have to understand that even if you fell prey to such superficial practices, I am not criticizing you personally. I am poking at a system of cognition in which such activity is deemed remotely valuable and rewarding. All of the first cognition is superficial, no matter how one operating there feels there is depth to a person. The perceptual world of the first cognition thrives on superficiality and image. It is the presentation and appearance that matters, not any real substance. The practices I just noted are part of that system of appearance and group acceptance. In all truth, such superficial renderings of ourselves in that manner is no different than the well to do exhibiting their own pretentious exteriors to their peers - putting on airs. Every ego is equally as pretentious to other egos in one form or another.

The sooner you can recognize how superficial that whole system of cognition is, the better off you will be where your cognitive advancement goes. Your quest is to find the real you, the *genuine* you inside, and get past the superficial overlay of your own ego and its habits that have been indoctrinated into you your whole life to make you functional in that superficial reality. When I instructed the readers in the first volumes of this series to actually question why they believe what they believe, this is a necessary element of that critical analysis for undermining the ego world of the first cognition.

The first cognition ego personality is predicated on beliefs and hopes, not truth and actuality. In the first cognition, hope sells, compassion sells, pity sells. In the second cognition, all of these superficial qualities have no true value. This is one reason Nietzsche spent so much of his writing leveling his polemics at the system. It is the *system* that holds peoples' consciousness bound. Having said that, every person maintains the personal responsibility to remove themselves from that system, or else remain slaves to it. Most prefer slavery of the illusion over the freedom of truth. As they say, "Ignorance is bliss".

Some of you may have advanced enough that you already feel that you no longer walk in tune with the world around you. This feeling of having one foot in one world and one foot in another is a natural part of the transition into the second cognition. Everyone who advances feels it and no one is immune from this cognitive perceptual change that they are no longer fitting into the world they've known all their lives. If you are feeling this way, take heart, it is something that will eventually pass, although it may take a few years for the full transition out of the first cognition for the feeling to disappear. For those who have yet to experience this feeling of living in two worlds at once, rest assured that if you stay the course, you will experience it sooner or later. Neither myself, nor anyone I have worked with has not experienced this no man's land between the two types of cognition.

The more you move toward the second cognition, the more this sense of isolation and disharmony is going to increase. You will eventually reach a point where just interfacing with the egos in the first cognition as you have all your life, is far from pleasurable. You will find, as you move forward, that foot still in the first cognition will eventually be nothing more than a toehold, that you no longer want to be burdened with the inanities of people still deeply immersed in that world. You will find that dealing with people in all their varied forms of seeking ego attention is just too damned tiresome and tedious to want to continue it, unless there is an absolute need to do so. When you reach this point, you will become sort of reclusive, simply to maintain your own sanity in the face of such superficial ego insanity. This is the meaning of Nietzsche's quote at the chapter head. You will want to be alone to escape the mental ego sickness of the first cognition.

In time, as you move past the bottleneck of the hourglass, and start to expand more fully into the second cognition, the tediousness of the first cognition will not wear on you as much once you stabilize and start to grow in the second cognition. During the transition period, this aspect of your development is hard to navigate. Unless you have someone walking their own path with you, you will find no one with which you can share these sensory perceptions of what is happening inside yourself, for those operating in the first cognition have no measuring tool to even comprehend what you are going through.

During this transition period, one can feel very lonely and isolated, and that is another reason many people step off the path. They can't deal with the sense of isolation, which is an aspect of separating yourself from the herd mentality of the first cognition. In a sense, this internal feeling of disharmony and living in two worlds is comparable to going through some kind of drug withdrawal. Each of us has lived our lives in the perceptual world of the first cognition, and as such, it is the only world we know. To contemplate altering our consciousness out of the only perceptual world we know into one we don't know is scary to anyone. It becomes harder to deal with when we can find no source of information that can tell us exactly what is happening or why. Many people wind up on therapist's couches, trying to hang onto the world of the first cognition rather than knowing that these sensations are a natural part of the transition to enlightenment. This is why I say enlightenment is a destructive process. We have to deconstruct the old world before we can step into a new one.

Since your roadway to enlightenment is personal, one should naturally expect a sense of isolation from others. No one outside yourself operating in the first cognition can tell you exactly what you are feeling internally, nor can they tell you how to deal with it. At best, they may suggest therapy, which is no solution to what you are feeling as you move forward.

In one sense, we all want to hang on to the world we know and try to make spirit fit into that realm of perceptual cognition. Many want spirit to manifest on their terms, rather than adjust to the terms mandated by spirit to move into the second cognition. Any exercise that tries to bend spirit to the will of one's ego is doomed to failure. If you can move your ego aside, your spirit is quite capable of helping you navigate your way into higher cognitive understanding. The hard part for everyone is not only the ego tyrant that rules our minds, but all of the perceptual notions we continue to embrace thinking they are truth. This is one of the major reasons that so few have advanced out of the first cognition throughout human history. The ego demands what it does on its terms. Your spirit does not cater to the demands of the petty ego, although it will let the ego rule you until you can find the means within yourself to fight it and start listening to your spirit self.

When you experience that sensation of having a foot in two different worlds, it is an indicator that you are progressing. You will realize this feeling even while your ego is still in control. Setting aside the ego is not a prerequisite for that spirit part of you inside to start exercising a certain amount of influence in your life if you stay the course to understanding with unbending intent to succeed. It is going to take time to discover and resolve this internal conflict between your real self and the ego fiction. Your spirit self is not as assertive as the ego, with the exception that this inner knowing one has that something more exists arises from your spirit more than originating with the ego.

When you feel that internal drive, what I refer to as a *push,* what Nietzsche called the will to power, it is one of your spirit's not so subtle nudges. Your spirit self wants out from under the tyranny of the ego. Your spirit knows you are more, even if your ego-ruled consciousness has not yet figured that out yet. So the ego gets pacified with chasing spiritual rainbows, while your spirit self *pushes* you to discover more. If you do not have this internal push to know, if your quest for knowledge is only for intellectual understanding, then it is your ego, not your spirit controlling your learning experience.

Everyone I have worked with who has advanced into the second cognition has this internal push. I have worked with others whose ego's imaginations are captured by ideas about spirit, but they never developed the internal push to break through into greater understanding. In time, their faddish fascination, based on their ego desires, leaves them and they go back to dawdling with spirit rather than truly advancing themselves, or they simply walk away from spirit studies and fall back into their old lifestyles. This is one way to explain the difference between the true seeker and the spiritual tourist.

The ego is a defender of perceptions. When an ego gets resolved to an idea, it is very hard to steer it way from that belief. I have seen no shortage of so-called spiritual seekers professing to seek truth, when in actuality, they are only seeking what their ego has convinced them is the truth. This is how people get roped into belief systems. Their ego convinces them that this is the way to go, and once convinced, they close their ears and their minds to anything that conflicts with that belief. They claim to be open-minded, for that is what is expected in the spiritual social setting, but when put to the test of professed open-mindedness, their close-mindedness exhibits itself, contrary to their claim of being open-minded. To progress on the path to the second cognition, one has to be honestly open-minded. One can't give simple lip service to the concept, as most people are wont to do, then remain rigid in their assumed belief structure and be honestly open-minded at the same time.

To progress into the second cognition, one must learn fluidity of perception. One can't hold onto faulty presumed truths when met with overriding or greater truths. One has to be cognitively fluid enough to change directions when spirit leads one to an alternative that is more realistic than the weak perceptual truths of the first cognition. It is through being fluid in this manner that the paring down of that hourglass takes place.

To be fluid does not mean to take everything one discovers in their research as gospel. If you are truly open-minded, your spirit self will tweak you with the truthfulness of many things. Sometimes these tweaks of realization result in the discomfort of cognitive dissonance described in the previous works. When one gets that overwhelming sense of cognitive dissonance, it is best to pay attention to what is revealed, for the chances are they are truths you need to acknowledge. Other things you research that only feel like might-be's, without that internal fear reaction generated by cognitive dissonance, are best either ignored or set aside as possibilities.

The spirit side of you knows truth. The hard part of acknowledging such truths resides with the resistance of ego programming. No one wants their world perception shattered, but to advance one's consciousness, that deconstruction is a literal mandate for advancement. It is often very uncomfortable. Certain instances of cognitive dissonance can't be resolved in just a few minutes. Sometimes it takes us days to come to terms with the shattered perception the truth reveals to us. None of these bouts of cognitive dissonance are pleasant. They were hard on me and those I worked with and they will be equally hard on you, but none of them are fatal. I can tell you that the more of it you deal with, the stronger you get and the less time it takes to bounce back from the emotional upset caused by such dissonance.

I can't give you a specific list of what pieces of information are going to rattle your world of perception because everyone's perceptual world is different. Some hang on to certain ideas more fervently than others, so what rattled my cage may not rattle yours, or anyone else's. This is another reason the spirit path can be so frustrating, because there is no procedural handbook that covers every aspect of what one must do as they move forward. The best I can do is tell you what to expect as you encounter whatever it is that you believe and eventually find out is wrong. The reactions are the same in everyone, but the particular stimulus that causes the reaction of cognitive dissonance is different in everyone. Also, the magnitude of the reaction depends on how deeply held a belief structure is. Often times, the fear jolt of realization is so powerful that it drives people from their paths altogether. To admit the truth is too overpowering for some to admit or deal with. It is exactly due to this type of predictable behavior that Leon Festinger was able to put forth *A Theory of Cognitive Dissonance* and have it accepted as a viable psychological theory. Everyone is subject to it. The only thing that is the variable is the manner in which each person deals with it. Certain 'weak' personality types are going to have a harder time than a stronger personality type.

Chapter 4

"Spirit is the life that itself cuts into life; by its own agony it increases its own knowledge --- did you already know that?"

Friedrich Nietzsche - Thus Spake Zarathustra

The path to your own cognitive advancement comes at the cost of a lot of psychological adjusting. The price to the second cognition does create a great sense of internal emotional agony as we confront our ego and its habits over the lengthy period of transition. A part of us must 'die' in order for a greater part of us to live. The ego program is what must die in all of us, and as it dies, so must its world of perceptual illusions.

Few people understand what this death of perceptual illusions entails. They feel that if you tell them the world is an illusion, that reality in matter will fail to exist. The world of matter exists, no matter how much quantum physicists theorize that in actuality it doesn't. The world of the material is not going to go away. You are still going to have to deal with the material world, meaning that if you bump your head on a tree branch, it is liable to hurt. Matter is not a perceptual illusion, for the most part. It is what we *believe* that makes our perceptual reality. Believing something doesn't make it so, it simply means a part of our cognitive system accepts the belief as true.

One of the major perceptual beliefs in the first cognition is that we can be guided by our emotions, that our emotional reactions are justified and wholly our own. Yet this is simply not true. Every human emotion, as it is used in the first cognition by our egos, is a reactive emotion, and the reaction is usually prompted by an ego responding in defense of preserving one of its deeply held perceptual illusions. Although one may set their ego aside, if they used the process described in *Demystifying the Mystical,* the ego is not necessarily permanently put away, at least not in the beginning. The ego program will readily jump back off that shelf if it is invited, so it takes a lot of mental discipline to insure it stays there. In saying this I have to issue a precaution in that regard.

I have seen more than one person who had the initial setting aside of the ego occur, only to have it come back off the shelf. In most cases when this happens, the person finds themselves playing mind games with their egos, playing like a game of hide and seek with the ego in their heads. This engagement of hide and seek becomes a counterproductive distraction to one's advancement. I have met no shortage of spiritual people engaged in this game of nonsense, with egos describing battles with their egos, all the while their egos are running them in circles. I ask that you don't fall for this game as it is more common than you may think. They get completely distracted by this mental game of hide and seek and usually lose all sight of their goal of spirit.

When you set your own ego aside, don't keep revisiting it through doubt. If you experienced the physical sensations of putting it in place, then accept that the process worked and focus on other areas of your development. If you keep playing with it, the likelihood of it jumping off the shelf is greater than if you accept you have completed the task and move on to addressing other parts of your advancement. Residual ego habits prompt one to keep poking at it, and the poking is all the excuse necessary for your ego to get right back into the game. I know all this sounds weird, but until you either have it happen to you, or observe it in others, you can't really fully comprehend the idea.

This leads us to a very important subject for discussion, and a question that every reader will pose, and that is - how does one tell the ego from an ego habit? There is a subtle distinction and I will do my best to describe it for you.

All our lives we have been programmed, not only with our thoughts, but through emulation of emotional reactions and behaviors we see in others. As babies we observed how adults used emotions, and not too long after we hit the cradle, we learn to start copying those same emotional reactions we observe in our parents. Over time, we all learn to operate by using our reactive emotions in response to virtually every situation we encounter. We develop the habit of how to exhibit anger when our ego feels justified in using anger. We learn how it feels to be depressed, and how to emotionally feel and exhibit joy. All of these emotionally reactive situations are the habits the ego adopts to become a participating member of the first cognition.

If you think about it, everyone exhibits emotions the same way. We learn to interpret others through their emotional displays, and in like kind, we use the same emotional reactions to express the pleasure or displeasure of our own egos. You can set your ego aside, yet you have a lifetime of these emotional reactive habits that are still in force after the ego program is set aside to go dormant. These emotional programs are what one needs to transcend in order to move into the second cognition.

I explained in the previous works that what some call spiritual balance comes about as a natural progression into higher consciousness. This state of balance, or stoic equanimity, only comes about when we can transcend all those embedded ego emotional habits and reactions. This is one area that cell talk can be used to one's advantage. As I said in the other works, although you may have your ego set firmly on that shelf, you still carry the residual emotional programming that has to be overcome to attain balance. Many people who have set the ego aside have an outburst out of programmed emotional habit and think the ego has jumped off the shelf, not realizing that it is an embedded programmed emotional reaction that came about through a lifetime of using those habits. This is what I mean by residual ego habits. We react due to the emotional habits we have developed as a nature of functioning in the first cognition. Old habits die hard, especially where emotional reactions apply.

One of those I worked closely with over the years noted that before their ego was set aside, the internal voice in their head egged them on during their emotional reactions. Once the ego was set aside, that internal voice stopped egging them on and all they had were the residual programmed emotional responses. You may note a similar difference in yourself as a form of detecting the actions of the ego compared to residual programmed ego-emotional responses.

Don Juan noted that no matter where you go, if you remove the veneer of cultural differences, every human reacts the same way as any human anywhere on the planet to the same stimuli. Granted, there is like a multiple choice list of reactions to any situation, but the list is not that long and it is highly predictable to anyone who has moved into the second cognition. The reason we have this predictable list of reactions is due to the reality framework of the first cognition. All such emotional reactions and outbursts are the same because that is the operating rules of all egos within the first cognition. Through enculturation, all humans in the first cognition exhibit the same limited range of emotions to any given stimuli, and they are always reactive, not emotionally pro-active.

In a reactive emotional state, you are never in control. You are always under the enculturated control of the first cognition. We all act the same because we are all taught the same rules of the game to the first cognition. Our egos have been shaped by other egos who react the same as we do, and it has been the same for humans throughout time. To move into the second cognition is to break these old ego habits, and it is not an easy thing to undertake or do. The reason that these habits can't be broken by most people is because we all assume it is a natural state for humans because everyone does it. They call it human nature, but it is not inherently human nature, it is only the nature of the habits of the first cognition. Those operating in the first cognition *assume* it is human nature because it is all they know - it is their *only* point of reference and interpretation. They can't see outside those perceptual boundaries to understand that it is not human nature at all, but it is in actuality *ego nature*. Once one progresses firmly into the second cognition, these accepted definitions are insufficient to describe the behavior of that second cognition person. The ego reactions that are used to define human nature are altered when one reaches the second cognition and attains balance. With the advent of balance, emotionally charged reactions by the ego disappear in the individual. In this respect, their actions are not the same as the herd and they can't be classified with the herd because their own internal nature has moved away from such predictability.

When one finally attains balance in the second cognition, first cognition egos feel uncomfortable when we no longer react to emotional stimulus the same way ego emotionally-reactive people do. They fail to get the expected emotional response that they do from others operating in that realm of perception, so we make them feel uncomfortable because we do not give their egos the desired or expected response that any other ego-reactive person will give them. We do not automatically respond to their ego's demands for attention or sympathy as does everyone in the first cognition. They find our demeanor of balance disconcerting.

Another aspect of ego habits is found with the internal dialogue. Although we may have the ego firmly emplaced on that shelf in our minds, the ego habit of talking to, or constantly thinking to ourselves in our heads takes a long time to wind down. Even if you are still prey to the internal dialogue, you must remember that it is embedded ego habit, and like any habit, it takes time to break the habit. When you find yourself engaged with the internal dialogue, it is often best to notice it and do something proactive to stop the running train of thoughts. Yes, this can be hard, but all of the work to get to the second cognition takes a form of discipline that the ego lacks.

I was a great thinker when I was in the first cognition. I thought all the time. I was so good at it that I could hardly stop the thought train long enough to get to sleep at night. I was always worried about something, or playing out fictional scenarios in my mind of what might happen if certain things occurred. My internal dialogue was a real champ! Some people's minds are more active in that regard than others, but everyone falls prey to the internal dialogue, especially when we find ourselves worrying about something. I don't know what it is about the ego, but it seems to love to worry - about anything. Once the wheels of worry are engaged, we can barely think of anything else except what we are worried about.

As I have said previously, worry is the greatest expenditure of energy that a human can engage themselves in, and it rarely bears any real fruit in the long run. As you have progressed on your path of enlightenment, many of you find yourselves worrying over whether you are ever going to get this spirit stuff at all. The sense of worry can and does drive some people from the path, and they fail themselves in the long run.

As I progressed on the spirit path, I quit more than once with the feeling that I was simply pissing up a rope where all this spirit stuff was concerned. I felt that I would never get it, and more than once became disenchanted with the process. But the spirit part of myself wouldn't let me drop it, so I always returned to the pursuit of understanding. If you have experienced this, then you know exactly what I am talking about. If you have not experienced it, maybe some of the explanations in these books will help you avoid such internal conflict and help you stay the course without so much personal disenchantment along the way.

Much of this disenchantment finds its source in the lack of valid information available on the subject. I never found any literature that plainly stated the pitfalls of the spiritual journey. After searching for so many years through different areas of research, and finding few cogent answers for what I was trying to achieve, I felt defeated that I would ever find any answers. I have talked with so many others on their path who have settled on whatever spiritual philosophy will purportedly help them achieve their goals, and I find that most are convinced that spirit is something it's not. Many of them get somewhat disenchanted and simply shift beliefs from one spiritual school of thought to another, thinking they will find answers by taking a new

37

direction. Such behavior only waste ones time looking for answers where none are present.

I am not holding myself above others when I relate these stories. The truth is that I was just as gullible and just as misdirected in what I *thought* spirit was about as everyone else. Like everyone else, I fabricated a mental illusion of expectations about spirit, none of which ever turned out to be true. I am relating these experiences so you know that if you have done the same things (and you probably have), to not beat yourself up over admitting that you did. You have to be honest with yourself in acknowledging these things. If all that is out there is partial truths mixed with a lot of speculation, we have nowhere to turn for answers other than fanciful imaginings. This is the picture that all spiritual pursuits paint in the world of the first cognition. Spiritual teachings put forth the idea that a spiritual master is somehow the next best thing to divinity. Most of the spiritual teachings out there can barely resist using the term *divine* to describe what you are seeking. It is no wonder that we all buy into that illusion of spirit when everything in the marketplace points in that one direction.

Believing in the divine is just another trap of the ego consciousness that makes it seek a higher form of external approval for its existence, or to delude themselves that they are somehow part of that divinity. This was explained in the previous books in this series. Giving rise to a belief in the divine automatically makes one a lesser being in their own minds. It is a trick as well as a need for the ego to find authoritative justification for its very existence. There is no higher external authority than the concept of the divine in the first cognition. As a lowly mortal who holds a concept of the divine, we make ourselves slaves to that mentality and also cheapen our spirit's real value to the lesser value of the ego.

You do not need any kind of divine source to validate the existence of your spirit self. In time, you will learn that all concepts of divinity are false interpretations of first cognition egos trying to explain what the great teachers tried to explain to them. The concept of the divine is a corruption that only sells to the limited cognition of an ego personality. This body of work is designed to help the reader clear the table of all such unrealistic and unnecessary beliefs predicated on dependency of the divine. The concept of divine guidance removes one from the responsibility for being accountable only to themselves and for their own actions. Such dependency is expressed when an ego asks, "Why is God doing this to me?" That is nothing more than a plea from an ego wrapped in its own self-pity seeking to blame God.

The ego begs God to fix its rotten life when it encounters bumps in the road. It wants God to fix it rather than fixing it for themselves. This is why I call the mindset of divinity nothing more than a dependency program. If enough people pray hard enough a situation may change. It is never conceived that the energy put forth through focused prayer (intent) may aid someone in their healing process, it is always presumed to be that God listened to their prayers and that is what made the difference. A miracle! One may not use the word God, but may choose instead to use the more amorphous term divinity, but the concept of a higher level source from outside ourselves amounts to the same form of mental dependency.

You are invited to move away from all such dependency thinking, whether you are dependent on God, the divine or the government. We each have to take responsibility, not only for our actions, but for discovering who we truly are buried underneath all these perceptions of our egos.

Chapter 5

"To lure many from the herd -- for that have I come. The people and the herd shall be angry with me: Zarathustra wants to be called a robber by the shepherds."

Friedrich Nietzsche - Thus Spake Zarathustra

Virtually every belief system in the first cognition seeks more adherents. They want converts from one form of doctrine to their form of doctrinal acceptance. This is why we have religious strife to this day around the planet. I have nothing to convert you to except knowledge of the real you inside. I have no doctrine to project, no dogma to proselytize and sway you to believe. Within the herd mentality labels abound - I am a Republican or Democrat; a Muslim, Hindu or Buddhist; an Atheist or a Christian, and the list goes on. Each of these labeling conventions serve as a source of identity for each individual ego. The label becomes part of their personality identification and a bastion for justifying all they believe and who they are.

I have no further needs for the labeling conventions of the herd. I am none of the above, as my own identity does not require the label of others to justify its own existence. If you express this to any religionist, their automatic assumption is that you must be an Atheist. Granted, I profess no belief in any God, but the label of Atheism is just as doctrinal as any religious belief. If one needs to label themselves as anything as a form of identifier to make them a different subset of the herd mentality, they are still subject to their own ego's need for justification through this labeling process.

As Nietzsche related in the chapter header, like him, I am here to guide people away from the herd mentality. I invite every reader to jump ship and become something more than they previously imagined. To an ego, this invitation to become something more leads to the erroneous conclusion that I place myself on some kind of pedestal to elevate me above them, to project the idea that I am somehow *better* than their own ego perceives them to be. What I want to impress on all readers of this material is that I am no better than any person on this planet. I will however qualify that by truthfully stating that I see things more clearly than most who are still captive to the herd mentality. Advancing into the second cognition gives one greater clarity and more far-reaching understanding than that offered in the first cognition. For a simple comparison, ask yourself who has a better view, one on the mountain top or one who is down in the swamp? What the second cognition offers to everyone who arrives there is a form of vision to see further than you ever have in the first cognition.

The ego personality can't tolerate the idea that anyone is better than its own self-image. It is part of its cognitive defense mechanisms. To prove this you only need to reflect on how many times in your life you have had people ask you, or you have asked others, "What, you think your better than me?" To advance into the second cognition, all such ideas need to be transcended. So long as you harbor the idea that you are better than others, or they are somehow better than you, your ego is still in place. Your cognition may be sharper and you will be able to see much of the ego nonsense for what it is, but your spirit self is no better than the spirit selves of others who still lie buried in the ego illusion. My criticisms are leveled at that system of cognition, not at any specific individual who may still be lost in that cognitive quagmire.

I explain this in order for the true seeker to recognize the ego habits within themselves. If you find that you have some kind of attitude of superiority over those who have not yet transcended themselves out of that system of cognition, then it is your ego giving you that perception. You have to develop a sense of humility in the face of greater understanding.

I don't have the right to judge or criticize a person for who they are, but I retain the right to question and judge the actions of their egos. Inside, each person has that hidden spirit self. In some it cries to get out from under the mental tyranny of the ego. In others, that drive is not present. You will save yourself a lot of inner angst if you learn to just let people be and don't try to criticize them as a form of external pressure to bring them to your way of thinking. Yes, it is a sad commentary on the state of humanity, but as you progress into the second cognition, you are going to discover just how hard this progression is. You don't need the additional worry about whether others get it or not. You are not their messiah any more than I am. You have enough to do just cleaning your own house without worrying about cleaning theirs as well.

And this brings us to impeccability. I use the word impeccability because it is more powerfully expressive than integrity. Integrity is subjective. In the first cognition one may have absolute integrity in protecting their belief systems, whereas impeccability is an obligation to one's own self-advancement. One can have extreme integrity and not have an ounce of spiritual impeccability.

Through my own experience and practices I always emphasize impeccability. Those most devoted to advancing themselves engage in the thought process of how to not violate others. Some feel that even mentioning what you are doing on your spirit path to someone else somehow violates your personal spiritual impeccability and invades their space. This is not the case. If, however, you turn into a proselytizer and criticizer of another person because they do not agree with you, you are violating your own impeccability. You violate impeccability by trying to force your views on another, and that violates their space. I am not violating my own personal impeccability by presenting these books, because I am not forcing my views on anyone. I am presenting information that anyone who reads these books has the ultimate personal choice to read them or not. I am not forcing my views on anyone, these views are sought out by the reader.

The ego personality rarely hesitates to insult another as a form of defense for its own actions. If you find yourself being confrontational in that regard, it is an ego failure and utterly lacks impeccability. The ego makes everything personal. Even in writing these books, although they were generalizations, many reader's egos took what I wrote personally. That is the nature of the ego, to personalize everything, and feel the need to defend itself even if it is not directly or personally challenged. If you feel that you have to defend what you believe about the second cognition, it is the standard ego reaction of the first cognition. If you find yourself still being defensive in that nature, this is a work area for you.

I have had encounters in online chat rooms trying to express the ideas presented in these books, and I have mostly been met with scorn, ridicule and blatant personal name calling by others. I find such exhibitions of ego personalities to be more the rule than the exception. I take none of their taunts personally because I have surpassed the ego need of feeling hurt or defensive. You may not yet understand how you can be this way, but when you develop the detachment necessary to remove yourself from the first cognition, all such emotional displays of ego defense are nothing more than examples of why humanity needs to transcend that mindset. It is not unlike a child throwing a temper tantrum because they can't get what they want. Such an exhibition *is* mentally childish.

The ego mind strikes out in order to hurt others, to denigrate them, and every response it gives is equally emotionally charged. By denigrating others, the ego makes itself feel superior. In the realm of the first cognition, every ego is on guard against being emotionally raped in that regard. Every ego has a hair-trigger switch for defense just waiting for someone to trip it. On the road to the second cognition, you are invited to get past all such ego mechanisms of defensiveness. When I say I have no emotional investment as to whether any reader gets this material or not, it means that I have transcended all ego need for validation from others. I have removed from myself all the expectations on which the ego thrives. I have developed the wisdom to know that those who will get the message will get it, and the rest are not my concern. I am not in any kind of emotional competition with the naysayers, nor do I feel any emotional need to defend myself in the face of their criticisms.

Such an attitude of emotional detachment is completely foreign to one operating in the first cognition. One is expected to have certain beliefs and they are expected to emotionally defend those beliefs like everyone else. What I am educating the reader with is not just another belief system. I am introducing you into a whole new way of life, a whole new way to view the world around you. This is not simple belief, and those who reach this goal will see it as I do, not because they believe me, but because it will reveal itself to them.

Impeccability amounts to maintaining the focus to push forward against all odds, both internally on a psychological basis, as well as getting past the need for external validation by other people. Impeccability requires one to be utterly and totally honest with themselves. We have to have the courage to admit our shortcomings and work to overcome them, not simply ignore them. That is impeccability.

It takes time to unravel the maze of beliefs we have each embraced as the boundaries of our own individual perceptual world in the first cognition. Sometimes this peeling away seems to happen in rapid succession, at other times you may find yourself with months between any happenings of this nature. There is no set flow that dictates any kind of timetable as to how this all unfolds for each of us. You are going to have to be patient with the process. You are going to have to be patient with yourself. No amount of ego-driven will power will make you advance any faster than your spirit self decides.

When we have the erosion of our beliefs and the bouts of cognitive dissonance, internally our consciousness has to make adjustments. These adjustments are not just found in getting past the immediate round of cognitive dissonance. It takes time for the new concepts to take hold and percolate. This is what I call the process of assimilation. We all have to mentally shift gears when our perceptual boundaries alter. It takes time to ponder on what the new information means to us in the grand scheme of our spiritual development. These periods of cognitive assimilation can take a long time.

You are going to feel down times, where it seems that you are not advancing at all, that no matter what you do you can't get unstuck in your process in order to advance. This happens with everyone. It is what I call a spiritual doldrum. In our Western societies, particularly with the advent of high-speed technologies, we have become accustomed to instant gratification. We want results and we want to see them now. This desire for fast results in matters of spirit will not serve you, as your spirit progresses at its own pace. There is nothing your will power, nor your desire to move faster, can do to make this transition. Every ego is impatient to see results. I was no different, and I doubt most readers are any different. As I have stated before, you will learn patience in this process because you basically have no real choice in the matter.

You are working to move your spirit self into the driver's seat where your ego has sat your entire life. The last thing your spirit self wants to do is so overload your cognitive circuits that you are not able to function in either system of cognition. Your spirit knows what you can handle and what you can't, so you have to develop the trust in that part of yourself to set the pace as you advance. There is vastly more to the cognitive picture than you can yet imagine and your spirit self has to build a cognitive foundation that can withstand these changes as you develop. When I tell you that you have to trust the process, I am telling you to trust your spirit self in how this all unfolds for you.

I related in *Demystifying the Mystical* how I pushed myself for years trying to understand spirit, and how one day, in reading certain passages of the Don Juan teachings, I suddenly realized that I had an understanding of what I had been seeking.

It could have been any one of the few books on my own recommended reading list that prompted this awareness. But in retrospect, I could point to no single catalyzing event that caused this transition in cognitive awareness.

As you progress in deconstructing your own perceptual illusions of the first cognition, I will suggest that what leads to that rollover of one's consciousness awareness is more of a cumulative effect. The more you work to unravel the false perceptions and remove the emotional programming that keeps us blind to the second cognition, at some point, all these events build up to a sort of critical mass in which the rollover into the second cognition occurs. I think no one can point to any particular event or circumstance that brings about this preliminary epiphany of understanding. And that trigger point to the rollover will be different in every individual.

Granted there are some exceptions to this rule, near death experiences and other traumatic events that may serve as a catalyst to catapult one's spirit into a state of higher cognitive awareness, but even those occasions are more the exception than the rule. I don't suggest anyone pursue spiritual advancement through any kind of forced trauma, thinking it will provide some sort of shortcut to enlightenment. There are no shortcuts in the process of unraveling the ego programs inside you. The sooner you realize this, the sooner you can settle in for the ride.

There is too much suggestive material in the spiritual arena that leaves people with the false impression that a shift in consciousness is something of external manufacture. It isn't.

Every person who has advanced into the second cognition had to work for it on a personal basis. It is never just blithely given away -- to anyone. You are not going to get it by osmosis, thinking that by hanging around someone who is spiritually advanced that it will magically rub off on you.

Having written all the foregoing, you may find yourself confused, for on one hand I am telling you that there is nothing you can do through simple will power that will transition you into the second cognition, yet on the other hand I have told you that you have to work for it. This may seem like a contradiction in concepts, but in actuality it is not. Your ego-driven will power will not make this change come true for you, but you must learn to discipline your focus to continue in the absence of what seems to be not happening for you. You must maintain your spirit's will to power, despite not immediately seeing tangible results.

We all look for results on the path. These results, once again, generally arise from a state of ignorance of not knowing just exactly what we are looking for. Here again, the problem of preconceived notions and expectations enters into the picture. We each dream up ideas about how we think spirit should appear in our lives. On my own path, I failed in thinking that certain abilities or gifts should be the same for everyone. I was envious and felt cheated because I did not have conversational interface with my guides. I got frustrated and whined and bitched about how unfair it all was. I lost many years pursuing these wrong ideas. In all that time I was yearning for the abilities of others I knew, and worked tirelessly to make those skills manifest in me through ego will power, and it never happened. I was so ego focused on being envious and trying to get the gifts others had that I completely overlooked my own spiritual talents. I wasted a lot of time in this effort, and spent years chasing phantoms of preconceived notions that never panned out. All the while I was missing everything about myself.

Chapter 6

*"It is time for man to set himself a goal. It is time
for man to plant the germ of his highest hope.
His soil is still rich enough for it. But that soil will
one day be poor and domesticated, and no tall
tree will any longer be able to grow in it"*

Friedrich Nietzsche - Thus Spake Zarathustra

One of the primary problems with working one's way into the second cognition is that you can only go so far before the information just flat runs out. In order to keep progressing, we all need information. One of the things that aggravated me most about the material available in the spiritual marketplace is that the majority of it just ran me in circles. Certain authors elevated themselves as if they had some kind of inside edge on spirit, claiming to have achieved enlightenment, and making lots of money doing seminars and writing books that the hungry egos sucked up by the millions. Many of them claimed to channel certain entities, and virtually all the channeled messages presented the same puzzle pieces with the channeler's own spin on the same tired old information. The words were different from one to the other, but in the end, the message amounted to the same type of pap to soothe egos - love, light and happiness.

Naturally, love, light and happiness sells, but the truth of the matter is that none of those feel good propositions will move one into the second cognition. They are doctrines that appeal to hungry egos trying to find meaning in their life, and everyone is a sucker for ego-oriented perceptions of emotional love and happiness, even if it is cloaked as some form of spirituality. Through the many years of pursuing my own understanding, I never caught this spiritual 'love bug'. Don't doubt for a second that I didn't try to tap into this purported divine source of love, happiness and cosmic unity that so many profess in the new age spiritual arena, but it never felt right to me from an intuitive standpoint. It felt too contrived. In retrospect, I see that as a positive event for my own development. Had I really caught the new age love bug, I might be as lost now as I was when I started my own quest. I would probably have wound up being just another drone in the army of the spiritually uninformed, chasing rainbows and butterflies to no positive end.

Most people start their spirit quest for all the wrong reasons. Many are egos who are simply seeking acceptance in the newest club, the social circles of the spiritual name droppers who spend inordinate sums of money to go see certain new age gurus speak. These people feel that they are somehow spiritually advanced because of the names they drop of who they met, etc. This type of person is the same kind of gadfly that chases movie stars and celebrities trying to validate their own *specialness* because they met John Travolta or Frank Sinatra. It is their own ego's claim to fame, but it doesn't make them in the least spiritual.

Many others are often prone to getting involved with crystals and high-dollar singing bowls. They feel that if they carry the accoutrements of the social club, that they are being more spiritual. I am not here to deride positive use of crystals, for they do have their value, but too many new agers feel that if they have a bigger crystal cluster than anyone else, or that they paid five times the value of a stone just because they got it in Sedona or some other new age Mecca, it makes them more spiritual than their club members. All of these traits just listed are as shallow as the ego of anyone else in the first cognition. Their egos have deluded them into thinking the trappings move them closer to spirit. In truth, they are just deceiving themselves and not moving one inch closer to spiritual understanding. All of these actions are performed by people who think that having the toys or dropping the names will bring them spiritual understanding through that process of osmosis mentioned above. It won't, it is just their egos jerking them around and deceiving itself with its own feelings of smugness.

I bring these observations up to inform anyone who may be involved in these superficial practices that you are only spinning your wheels if you think such activity means a whit on the real path to self-advancement into the second cognition. I have met all varieties of these people in my years of advancing myself. Their pretentiousness gives true spiritual pursuit a bad name, and that is why most aspects of spirit are deemed woo-woo by the more 'realistic' aspects of first cognition society.

In many respects, much of the new age movement appears to be a 60's hippie revivalist movement more than it has anything to do with spirit. In the neo-pagan communities, as well as the new age, you will find many people taking hallucinogenic drugs on a regular basis claiming that they are seeking enlightenment through using DMT and other substances. I discussed in *Demystifying the Mystical* just why such approaches to spiritual advancement are doomed to unreliable misinterpretations and failure. They use books like Rick Strassman's *DMT: The Spirit Molecule* as the foundation for their belief that taking drugs will take them to enlightenment.

Strassman's interpretation of the effects of DMT to produce some kind of mystical effect shows how misdirected he was in his own interpretation - once again trying to describe spiritual advancement as something mystical. Whatever DMT may or may not do to the human brain, it is not mystical. It produces a chemical synaptic overload that creates the 'visionary' experience which some people interpret to be mystical. Graham Hancock, in his own research, and in an attempt to contact his dead father, went to the jungles of South America seeking his own brand of mystical revelation using a brew made from the *ayahuasca* plant, the active ingredient of which is DMT. His story is catalogued in his book *Supernatural*. He didn't achieve his mystical goal, even after repeated attempts of taking the drug.

I am here to tell the reader that at no time since I started my own quest for spiritual understanding did I ever have to resort to hallucinogenic drugs, or any other type of drug to get any form of enlightenment. In fact, I found the more I progressed on my path, they less I liked any substances that messed with my mental clarity - beer included - and I used to be an avid beer drinker for many years.

Any experience produced by the ingestion of any foreign substance is unreliable. It may feel mystical while it is happening, and one may even feel that they saw something spiritual after the fact, but in the end, they will still be as firmly rooted in the first cognition as they were without the experience. Since the purported visions occur under the influence of a drug, whatever one sees is wholly unreliable as any type of gauge to spiritual understanding.

As the quote provided at the chapter heading suggest, you have to set your goals high. You have to set a goal that transcends all this need for the mystical and magical. You have to reach for the farthest star where your perceptual advancement is concerned. Never settle for second best along the way. Never buy the counterfeit presentation of real spirit that masquerades as mysticism.

To advance yourself you have to become inquisitive. You have to ask questions; questions to yourself if to no one else. From my own personal experience I have seen a lot of people sitting around saying that they are waiting for spirit to guide them. While they are waiting for this purported guidance, they are sitting in idle and moving nowhere. The reason I got where I am; the reason I am in a position to share this information, is because I never stopped asking questions. I still ask questions. I never run out of questions.

What I find most disappointing is with the people who have actual conversational contact with their spirit guides who never ask them a single question unless it relates to their romantic 3D affairs or how to get money. Spirit guides are with you to guide you in spiritual matters, not your everyday 3D life. They are not your social advisors for first cognition concerns. They are not with you to help you find your "twin flame' or to pick the winning lotto numbers. Most importantly of all, they are here to *guide* you through your spiritual quest, not *lead* you. So quit sitting around whining because your guides aren't telling you anything. Start being pro-active with them and start asking relevant questions about your spiritual development and see how much progress you make.

I don't have the gift of direct communication with my guides, but if I did, I would never leave them alone through my constant questions. As it is, I do have a certain mode of communication with my guides, but it is very subtle and it took me many years to figure out how their guidance worked with me. If you happen to be one of these types of people who has the gift of direct conversational communication, if you want to advance your spirit, then start asking your guides lots and lots of pointed questions so you can start to grow yourself. Stop sitting on your yazz waiting for them to serve you wisdom on a silver platter. If you want to know, you have to ask. You have to show a sense of self-motivation. Without that motivation, one's spirit guides are not in the least bit obligated to hold your hand while you do nothing to advance yourself. In actuality, guides are conscious beings like we are and being your guide is their job. By not allowing them to do their job or for you expecting them to do *your* job, it is very selfish and very far removed from spiritual impeccability.

Yes, my words are critical. But for Pete's sake, people, what do you think enlightenment is all about? If you are one of those people who I just called down, be humble enough to admit you made a mistake and move past it. Don't spin your wheels getting angry with me because I called you on your nonsense. If you are reading this material it indicates that you are at the least somewhat serious in advancing yourself spiritually. Take the information presented and make use of it. Don't sit around in self pity recriminating yourself for past mistakes. *Learn* from this!

I make the assumption that the majority of people reading this material are looking for something. Many are looking for answers to questions that no one else really seems able to answer, or you wouldn't be reading this material trying to find those answers. You may not like the answers you find here, but at least I am not dangling fanciful mysticism in front of your face to lure you down a dead end road. I told you that the spirit path is pragmatic. It requires a sort of common sense (although there is no real common sense). Call it a more down to earth approach to spiritual matters without all the fluff that passes itself off as spirituality in the marketplace.

Many of the observations I make in this book will make a lot of readers uncomfortable, or more accurately, it will make their egos uncomfortable. I don't care about your ego, or your ego's hurt feelings or your ego's self pity and defensiveness. Your ego is your problem, not mine. But I am not going to mollycoddle you with the truth just so your ego can feel good about itself. Your ego can hate me and run me down all it likes in order to try and preserve its control over your mind and your emotions. Every finger I jab is at your ego so you can hopefully learn how it manipulates you. I am not writing to your ego, I am writing to the spirit self inside you that is trying to come out.

The first cognition has run its gamut. There is no place else for it to advance. It is a sealed room of consciousness. Already we are so domesticated by the first cognition that the soil to the second cognition has grown thin. You have to decide if you can grow your own consciousness into a giant redwood tree of understanding, or whether you want to remain a twisted shrub dying of thirst and nourishment in the first cognition.

Chapter 7

"I tell you: one must still have chaos in oneself to give birth to a dancing star. I tell you: you still have chaos in yourself."

Friedrich Nietzsche - Thus Spoke Zarathustra

I want to make an observation and pose a couple of questions to the reader. We have thousands of years of mystical traditions, Buddhist, Hindu, Egyptian, Greek and many, many others that humans have leaned on over the centuries in order to find spiritual understanding. Have you ever bothered to think about the fact that after thousands of years of these varied traditions, why the so-called enlightened masters have not really move forward at all once they attained their moment of enlightenment? Why have none of them progressed beyond their instilled traditions to venture into the new territory of the second cognition?

I related how the Buddhists, as well as many others, seem to be stuck at the bottleneck of the hourglass, and none have progressed beyond that bottleneck to advance their knowledge once they arrived. For thousands of years they have refused to disembark from the plane. I used the illustration of how the top of the hourglass could be representational of the whittling away of the perceptions of the first cognition to reach that bottleneck into the second cognition. If the top of the hourglass represents the whittling away of the ego cognitive perceptions, then past the bottleneck, we have the chance for enhancing and growing our knowledge as we progress into an expanding bottom half of that hourglass. We have to ask why no one seems to have ventured much into that new territory. I have found only one source that did so, and that was Don Juan. By his own claims, the second cognition is not all there is, that beyond that is what he called the third cognition.

If this one teacher could relate this message, then why is it that so many other professed masters over the ages have not gotten off the plane of ancient traditions to embark into this new territory of consciousness? What keeps them all complacent to have achieved alleged enlightenment and not explore new regions of consciousness?

To advance into the second cognition is not to simply arrive. It means that you must progress deeply into it if you want a broader understanding of the universe beyond the doorstep of 3D. Yet all these presumed masters seem to not have ventured one step beyond the doorway they have open before them. They are all riding on the laurels of their ancestors and their traditional ways. They look backward in order to arrive, but having arrived, they do not look forward to discover more.

This author was not content to simply arrive. I have expanded my own knowledge and understanding by blazing a trail deep into the territories of the second cognition, and I continue to do so. Few have gone where I have mainly due to the complacency I just illustrated. I have advanced into an unexplored territory that awaits *anyone* with the drive to discover it for themselves. We have to ask ourselves if such broad vistas are available to us, why the so-called masters of all the esoteric and mystical traditions have not done the same thing? Why are they all still peddling the same mystical garbage?

I make these statements of fact, not to glorify myself, but to ask why others have not done the same thing in all the thousands of years of recorded mystical traditions? The option for pioneering research into the second cognition was available to them just as it was to me, and as it is to you. So why have they been stuck in the mud for so long?

The answer to this question appears to be that they were simply content to stay where they were. They had no inquisitiveness to seek understanding, because they presumed they already knew all they needed to know. Their mystical predecessors set the goal called *enlightenment*, and they were content to just get there, thinking that reaching the goal is all there was to it. On the other hand, I was not simply content to just get there. I knew in my gut there was more, and I was not to be satisfied until I discovered it. Even knowing what I know at this time, there is still more. As the adage goes, the more I know, the more I discover how little I know. It is this lack of knowing that drove me through all my years of cognitive advancement. It is what drives me to this day. You have to ask yourself if you have that same drive to know as I did, or if you are one who will be content with simply arriving and not getting off the plane.

If you advance and choose to get off the plane and start to explore, you are going to discover that there is no singular guiding intelligence to the universe. No matter how far out I reached and no matter how hard I pushed my own cognitive envelope, I only found other sentient beings trying to figure it all out like I was. I discovered that there was no such thing as a divine source for everything.

Just as Nietzsche said, you have to find the chaos within yourself if you want to grow and expand. Yes, the soil is thin and almost depleted in the first cognition, but from that soil mighty trees of cognition can still take root and grow. Every one of my books is meant to serve as the nourishment that helps such trees grow. You have already chosen to sow the seeds to your own advanced cognition. I am only providing the information to help clarify what you are seeking and what it takes to get there. As much as your ego protests at being poked at, your spirit is sitting on the sidelines cheering you on, waiting for the day that you are your spirit and the ego is nothing more than a distasteful memory.

These books are meant to serve as a rallying point of inspiration to your spirit self. Your ego hates what I am doing. It hates me for exposing what it is. But you have to recognize it if you ever hope to defeat it. I'm telling you what your spirit self already knows, that there is more to you than you can yet imagine. Let that revelation serve as an inspiration for you to go forward in the face of adversity. Let these messages serve to keep your spirit impassioned to continue on this quest, no matter how hard it seems at times. And you will have hard times.

I am now, cognitively speaking, beyond anything I could ever imagine in the first cognition. When I describe the painful circumstances that everyone encounters on this path, a question that is very often asked of me is whether I feel it was worth it, whether all the emotional pain and turmoil was worth what I got in the end. For myself, I have to be honest and answer that no matter what I had to endure to get here, I would endure that and even more to be where I am cognitively speaking. I feel I have lost nothing in comparison to the vistas that have opened up to me in the alternative.

Many people ask how I function with the second cognition living in a first cognition world. As I said previously, it is hard at first. The adjustment is hard to deal with, even when one finally achieves a sense of balance. But you have to try and understand this. Just as you whittled away the first cognition at the top of the hourglass, the longer you reside in the second cognition, the more your perception advances so long as you continually pursue greater understanding. You won't progress very far if you become satisfied and complacent.

I wrote the third book in the series first. At the time I composed it, my cognition had actually not advanced enough to write the second volume at that time. It was only months later that my awareness had advanced to the point I could compose *Willful Evolution* and present it in a cogent manner where first cognition people could understand it. That book took only six days to write. It was only a matter of a couple of weeks after I finished *Willful Evolution* that I was able to write *A Philosophy for the Average Man* in about 4 days.

Demystifying the Mystical took me a mere two weeks to write. It took a few weeks more to edit it, and after the first and second volumes were written and submitted for publication, I had to do a major edit/rewrite of *Demystifying the Mystical* in order to get it ready for public release. While I was fretting over the work required for that rewrite, I started writing this book.

The point I want to make in sharing this information, once again, is not to glorify me or gloat over how quickly I wrote these books, but to illustrate to you how once you get firmly operative in the second cognition (not still sitting on the plane), your cognition keeps advancing in understanding so long as you are not content to ride on your laurels. You will never see this type of advancing cognition in yourself if you only arrive and stay put at the bottleneck of the hourglass. Nietzsche wrote the first part of *Zarathustra* in only ten days. When the fruit of cognition is ripe, presenting it to others is the easy part. Waiting on the ripening process is what takes the longest.

You may wonder why I make the admission that I wrote the first three books in this series in reverse, yet presented them as a linear sequence from 1st to 3rd. If you have read the books, you already understand the reason for presenting them in the sequence I did. Each volume builds on the one before it, just as this volume naturally follows the others. But at the time I wrote each one, I did not have the cognitive *understanding* to present the principles in the manner that I did as a translator of those principles. I had knowledge about the matters I presented, but I had not yet advanced to a state of cognitive understanding to know how to translate the ideas where people operating in the first cognition could comprehend what I wrote. Once I had that understanding, the books wrote themselves.

By telling you this story it is hoped that you can get a glimmering of what the second cognition can do for you, and also why I wouldn't trade what it has brought me for the world. The messages in this series are sorely needed in a world that lacks any kind of real information on these subjects. I look back at the difficulties on my own path and I say, "Man, I wish I had information like this when I was searching for answers. It could have saved me a lot of years chasing shadows."

It is my desire that you find this information helpful on your own path. That is the only reason I am writing this series. It is not for fame or fortune. These books are being written for the simple reason that no one else is doing it, or apparently qualified to do it. They are written for the reader, not for the self-gratification or glorification of the author. By sharing all this information I am being impeccable in spirit. I could easily sit on this information and no one would benefit from it. My own impeccability demands that this information be released to the general public, just as I'm sure that Nietzsche's impeccability led him to compose *Zarathustra* and his later works. We both want to see humanity grow out of the emotional adolescence of the first cognition.

I wrote in an earlier chapter about that internal *push* that spirit provides to give us direction and impetus to things to advance ourselves. Every one of these books is a result of that *push*. If you move forward on your own path, you will become familiar with the push. I will advise you about a push. When you get a push to do something, pay attention to the push and act on it. The longer you delay on a push, the harder it will push you. Many pushes are time sensitive. For instance, if you get a tweak to go to the bookstore, and the tweak is accompanied by a push, don't make excuses not to go. Act on it when you get it. The harder you feel a push, the more urgently action is required. If the push is not a hard push, but feels more like a nudge, then you probably have a larger window of time to act on it. But the closer the window gets, the stronger the push will become. Many of you have already experienced pushes, so this information is not new to you. But for those of you who haven't yet felt a push, pay attention to what I am sharing. It is very important information. A push is your spirit self guiding to do or find something that you need in your life. If you ignore the push, you will never discover what that may be.

One final set of thoughts needs to be shared about pushes. Most of the time when spirit pushes you to take some kind of action, you don't get any specific indicators of exactly what you are being pushed to discover. The push could bring you into contact with other people, or help you find things you need or that you have expressed an intent to own. Spirit pushes *can* guide you to sales on products you have been seeking, believe it or not. This is one aspect of spirit and pushes, that you rarely know exactly why you are getting the push, you only know that you are and when you act on these pushes, most of the time you figure out what the push was about after you act on it.

It is very hard to explain what a push is. It is a feeling, but it is not associated with emotions. Virtually all of the second cognition is driven by such feelings. These feelings can be best illustrated by someone who gets a feeling of dread and chooses not to board a plane, only to have the plane crash. It is an intuitive sensory sensation not remotely associated with how the ego uses your emotions. It is a sixth sense. Not all of these sensory capabilities focus on the negative. A push is one of those sensory sensations that can't be described, but once someone feels a push, they know exactly what I am talking about. Learning to pay attention to these intuitive sensory feelings is how one navigates into and operates in the second cognition. This is why there is nothing in the first cognition that can remotely prepare you for operating in the second cognition.

Chapter 8

"Zarathustra is changed, Zarathustra has become a child, Zarathustra is an awakened one: what do you want now in the land of the sleepers?"

Friedrich Nietzsche - This Spake Zarathustra

I provided an exercise in *Demystifying the Mystical* to help attune yourselves to subtleties. The feelings of spirit I described in the last chapter requires that we develop the ability to be cognizant of the subtle nature of the second cognition. Unlike the first cognition which is always blaring and in your face, spirit in the second cognition works more through nuance and subtleties.

It is nigh onto impossible to describe how things work, perceptually speaking, in the second cognition. We have no comparative framework within the first cognition to explain or define the perceptual nature of senses that go beyond first cognition perceptions based on our primary five senses. I know that most readers are not going to understand what I am about to write. This is not an insult to your intelligence, it simply means that within the first cognition you have no point of relationship to comprehend it. It is completely foreign territory to most of the readers as it was to me when I was trying to understand it.

There are a few books I discovered on my spirit path that I found to be invaluable over time. In each of these books, the messages kept talking about following our feelings. From the interpretive standpoint of the first cognition, when we read about feelings, we have an immediate association with emotions, because that is our primary basis of understanding the word feelings when we hear it. In time, what I came to realize is that these teachers were not talking about emotional feelings at all, but were instead referencing the intuitive sensory feelings of the second cognition. I spent many years in confusion over this misunderstanding, especially once I achieved my own state of spiritual balance.

As you work to erode the tyranny of your own ego, and the reactive emotions it generates to protect it's world, those emotions are no longer the primary factor for interpreting your consciousness. Let me see if I can explain this better. As an ego-controlled first cognitioner, we react through our emotional center. Through a form of cellular programmed manipulation, the ego pulls forth these reactive emotions to protect itself. As you deprogram yourself from the wiles of the ego, these emotional reactions cease. When you reach that state of balance, you are basically pretty non-emotional in a reactive sense. This doesn't mean you don't have emotions, it means that you are no longer reactive in how they are abused by your ego. This was discussed in depth in *Demystifying the Mystical.*

Where my own confusion arose in reading the messages about paying attention to your feelings, was that removing reactive emotional responses from myself and gaining balance, interpreting that I should follow my feelings (emotions) made absolutely no sense to me. It seemed counterintuitive to attaining balance at all. I puzzled over this for quite a number of years before my cognition advanced enough that I finally got what they were talking about. The feelings we need to pay attention to are not our emotions, they are the *sensory feelings* of the second cognition!

In all honesty, I had developed my subtle awareness to a keen edge over the years, but I was still translating the word feelings from the first cognition definition of emotions. I had already developed a high skill in paying attention to my second cognition feelings, but my understanding, my *comprehension* of the message being related was being misinterpreted. I have told you in previous works that enlightenment is not a goal, but is an ongoing evolutionary process. When it finally dawned on me what the real meaning of feelings was in the context delivered by Don Juan and the other messengers, it was an epiphany. It was also sort of a flat forehead moment in the sense that I had utterly failed to comprehend its meaning before that moment of awareness.

I share this story with you to help you realize that you are also going to have moments of cognitive advancement that bring insights of comprehension where you lacked it before. This is also why I emphasize the difference between knowledge and understanding. With understanding comes comprehension. Many of you reading these books will walk away with knowledge. But you may not walk away with comprehensive cognitive understanding. It may take you rereading these books 6 months or a year down the road before the cognitive comprehension kicks in. When that happens, remember it, for that will be a gauge of your cognitive advancement.

Always keep a finger on where you came from on this journey. The only measure of advancement will be found when you compare how you are today to how you were a year ago, or five years ago, or even a month ago. If you don't remember where you started on your journey, remember your lack of understanding, then you will be hard put to see your own advancement. I have always worked to remember how I was when I started this journey. I can't recount every aspect of my development, but I remember enough to be able to gauge my own progress. You would be well advised to do the same. There may well come a time in your life that you become a guide or instructor to others. If you can't remember your own hardships, you will find it very hard to relate to those who still face such hardships on their own path. For those I have worked with on their paths over the years, I have always emphasized this remembering where you came from aspect for gauging one's own development.

Another area of misunderstanding that nearly drove me nuts over the years was Don Juan's teachings in *The Art of Dreaming*. Although Carlos Castenada put all his emphasis on the dream state itself, and fabricated his own stories of astral projection based on his misunderstanding, my own efforts in trying to perform what Don Juan taught gave me no end of frustration. For any of you readers who have struggled over the teachings in that same volume, let me take the time to clarify just what the hell Don Juan was talking about. Once again, this may go beyond your immediate level of comprehension, but what I am about to share is very important when it comes to navigating your way through the second cognition.

In order to clarify all this for everyone, but particularly those who have tried to understand Don Juan's teachings, I am going to cover two points that gave me no end of problems comprehending over the years. In most of the Castenada books, Don Juan talked about what he called the *assemblage point*. We are only left with what Castenada shared about his limited understanding of those teachings, and his personal fictionalized adventures only muddied the waters of understanding for millions who have read his books over the years.

The assemblage point is nothing more than a point of perceptual focus when you are venturing outward into the second cognition. The assemblage point, in a simple comparison, is like one of those fine point laser lights. The assemblage point is a focal point for pinpoint accuracy to read the varied frequencies of the second cognition. More explanation of these things will be related in subsequent volumes, but for now, just know that the assemblage point is the cognitive point of perception that we each have to develop in order to navigate the second cognition. To move the assemblage point is like changing the station on a radio dial or changing channels on a TV.

To understand what Don Juan meant by the term dreaming, you have to understand the cognitive focal point of the assemblage point. Although there are some who can engage in lucid dreaming, there is a higher level of dream work in the sleep state that can be willfully navigated by those who have a gift for it. As for myself, I never developed that particular talent in the sleeping dream state, but I know others that do.

In the course of teaching Castenada, Don Juan used the term dreaming while awake, or dreaming-awake. For years this terminology made absolutely no sense to me. After learning myself how to navigate within the second cognition, it finally dawned on me one day that everything I was doing, tapping into other-dimensional frequencies and perceiving what was going on there, is what he meant by dreaming. For those who have sought to understand what he meant by dreaming, this is it.

In the sleeping dream state, over the years I discovered that there are certain dreams that had a different 'texture', a different 'feel' than normal dreams. They were more vivid, more real than normal dreams processing subconscious garbage. I found that many of these dreams were what I call message dreams. I received certain information that I was supposed to retain, and after the information was delivered in the dream, I was prompted to wake up so I could remember the dream. All of these messages were not specifically clear. I often had to ponder on them to get the meaning of the messages. Sometimes, although delivered in a form of typical allegorical dream-speak, the messages were immediately understandable. Other times I had to ponder the dream for days before I could understand the underlying meaning, and other dreams I couldn't figure out at the message at all.

When working in the second cognition, we often get messages through dream communications. What takes time and some skill is learning to recognize message dreams from the other normal dreams. The second cognition works totally different than anything the first cognition prepares us for. When we step into the second cognition, just as the quote at the chapter heading reveals, we are all like a child. We have spent our entire lives bound in the first cognition, and all of our modes of interpretation are based on that first cognition knowledge. The perceptual rules that apply in the first cognition do not apply in the second cognition. When we enter the second cognition, we are all children when it comes to understanding the nature of the second cognition perception. When we enter the second cognition, there is no point of reference in the world of the first cognition 'sleepers' to guide you.

From the standpoint of the first cognition, everything I just related to you is impossible. To one roped into the first cognition, these revelations are merely flights of fancy, they can't possibly exist except in my own vivid imagination. To others it may still have the feel of being somehow mystical, but it is not mystical, it is wholly pragmatic in the second cognition. The deeper one moves into the second cognition, the better the understanding they gain in learning the rules of operation there. At first, we are all lost, feeling we don't know what the hell we are looking for nor what to expect. It is my desire that these books are removing some of that mystery.

As a word of warning though, just as we have difficulty with the top of the hourglass, learning to navigate through the bottom of the hourglass presents its own set of difficulties. As I explained, we have those experiences of cognitive dissonance as we remove the ego barriers. As you progress into the second cognition, you are going to find things that equally challenge any expectations or interpretations you may have about the second cognition. We all bring parts of the first cognition into the second cognition with us. Until we learn the ropes, all any of us can do is use first cognition perceptions to try and understand and interpret the second cognition. These primary perceptual interpretations are very often going to be turned on their heads. The universe is not what you think it is. The other intelligences you encounter out there are not what you may perceive them to be at this time.

We all know the feeling of moving up from elementary school to middle school, and from middle school up to high school, and from high school into college. At every one of those junctures in our lives, we went from being in the highest grades into the next institution at the lowest grades. Moving into the second cognition is more accurately compared to moving from kindergarten to college in one leap. In the grand scheme of the evolution of the universe, Earth humans are only a late arrival on the scene that is billions of years old. No matter how broad you think your perception is, no matter how intelligent you think you are, your perceptual world is going to be shaken to the core more than once as you move into the second cognition. This is not an idle observation, it is a fact that you need to take very seriously.

For 19 of the last twenty years I have been actively poking around the universe before I even understood fully what the second cognition was. If you have certain gifts, or know people who do, working in the top of the hourglass is no restriction to making contacts in other places off this planet. It is through many of these contacts 'out there' and their assistance and co-operation over the years that I finally came to many of the realizations that I am sharing in these books. I will freely admit that this was not the wisest thing to do, for it has cost me in numerous ways that I am going to cover later in this volume, but had I not ventured there at all, I would not have developed many of the tools I use, of which only a few have been shared in these works.

I am not going to devolve this volume into tales of science fiction and high adventure. I am only relating this stuff at all because it is necessary for your own understanding. What I have experienced and even more will be at your disposal if you follow a path even remotely similar to the one I did. What is presented herein is designed to explain most of the pitfalls that I experienced, as well as others I have worked with along the way. Granted, there may some personal variances, but what I am sharing is the things generally experienced by myself and all those I have worked with directly with as co-travelers on this road to awareness.

In truth, I hesitate to tell much of what I have experienced because it will give the scoffing sleepers too much ammunition to destroy the foundation I have built already. I don't fear their opinions, for none of what they may say will alter a single thing that I can relate. Too many others have been along with me on this path when the really 'spooky' stuff happened for me to accept it is a simple delusion or group hallucination. By spooky, I don't mean scary like a ghost story or horror movie, I mean spooky like Einstein defined quantum physics as 'spooky action at a distance'. Working to learn about the universe outside stark materialistic scientific interpretation can best be defined as spooky action at a distance.

There is absolutely no foundation in first cognition science to remotely explain how the universe actually works, and as such, any explanations about how it works contrary to their materialist conclusions is going to fall on uninformed deaf ears. The day I look forward to is the day that a qualified quantum scientist steps into the second cognition and realizes how hopelessly insufficient first cognition scientific tools are for describing the universe or understanding its workings.

I sense there is going to be scoffers at even the preliminary claims shared in this book, those who will challenge the idea that anyone on Earth can contact any other type of being in the cosmos without some form of physical device intervention or some kind of mystical experience. They will argue that the speed of light, at the very least, prevents any such contact in any realistic manner. From the standpoint of their limited perception, this is absolutely true. But as a challenge, science is in the business of measuring measurables, of quantifying quantum *particles*. All of their science is based on the presumption that everything in the universe is harnessed by our 3D perception. Even light particles can be quantified, and as such, the speed of light is the limit to speed from first cognition understanding.

If you look at even the parts of the universe we are just now getting a glimpse of through our most highly advanced telescopes, using the speed of light, or even FTL (faster than light) travel, is painfully slow when compared to the distances involved. Traveling at light speed, or even FTL, to find and contact more advanced races, can be compared to a horse and buggy in comparison to instantaneousness of thought.

Having made this observation, the reader has to be wondering just how it is that I have navigated any of the universe at all in order to glean any professed knowledge of its workings. The answer is blatantly simple. The universe is a vast network of information that any sentient being of higher level cognition can tap into once they develop the skill to use it. This same network serves as a conduit, not unlike a fiber optic network, through which thought travels instantaneously.

One doesn't have to fully step into the second cognition to make these types of contacts or experience such a mode of communication. It can be accomplished while one is still in the first cognition, and in truth, those who can directly communicate with their guides already have this ability to a certain degree.

The speed of thought puts the speed of light to shame. If you can develop your own cognitive skills highly enough, there is no barrier in reaching the vast reaches of this universe in an instant and communicating with other cognitively advanced consciousnesses. What will prevent any of you from discovering this for yourself is by setting up your own system of disbelief that such things are possible.

Whenever we deny any possibility, we shoot ourselves in the foot and it impedes our further advancement into understanding. With such self-imposed cognitive restrictions, your advancement will be slow and remain stalled until you remove the blinders of your limited acceptance. As I said, we all drag the measuring tools of the first cognition with us into the second cognition. These same tools, called beliefs, are what hamper anyone in learning anything.

I told you that you have to develop fluidity of thought and perception. The only reason I did any of the things I did is because I recognized very few restrictions to learning what I wanted to know. I pushed the envelope at every turn. When I felt the borders to the information I sought was restricted, I pushed more and pushed harder. I did not set up mental barriers of restriction. I did not limit myself any more than my lack of understanding presented at any given time. Whenever I felt I couldn't get somewhere to get the answers I sought, rather than saying "I can't", I asked the question, "Why can't I", and then I started searching for a workaround to the problem.

In finding the solutions to the multitudes of problems I faced on this journey, even before my consciousness rolled over into the second cognition, I had to think creatively. I had to become a creator to my own solutions. We are all creators in that regard, but you have to ask yourself, how much creating have you been doing along the way? This question is not leveled as a criticism, it is designed to help alter your mode of thinking. I have taught people for years that in order to advance you have to stop thinking like a human. Thinking like a human is all first cognition limited thinking. You will never find your answers to the great mysteries of the universe if you continue to use the first cognition as your measuring stick.

The reason I continued to advance is because when I encountered certain hurdles, rather than give up in defeat, I thought, "there must be a way around this", and I discovered that if I pondered the situation long enough a solution would eventually present itself. You can't stay defeated in the face of adversity or you will never advance. You can't become a self-created consciousness if you get frustrated and quit when things get tough. If you are wise enough, you will find a solution. Your spirit is much wiser than your human mind can yet comprehend. The information that is available through intuitive reckoning is beyond astounding. This is maybe a more poignant example of what I mean by *unbending intent.*

At the beginning of our journey we are all very distrustful of ourselves. We have all been raised in a cognitive system that operates from the ego insecurity of self-doubt. In order to work within the intelligent network of creation, you have to learn to trust yourself and trust your own intuitive instincts. Virtually none of us are prepared to function in that manner because the first cognition doesn't even recognize such a thing exists as a valid option. In that regard, we are all mentally hobbled when we are seeking understanding and spiritual advancement. We are all dragging the ball and chain of the first cognition around with us every step of the way until we can release ourselves and finally stop thinking like a first cognition human.

Chapter 9

*"All that is unfamiliar in the future, and whatever
makes stray birds shiver, is truly more familiar
and cozy than your "reality".
For thus you speak: "We are wholly real and
without belief or superstition": thus you thump
your chests--ah, even with hollow chests.
Indeed, how would you be **able** to believe, you
many-colored ones! -- you who are pictures of all
that has ever been believed."*

Friedrich Nietzsche - Thus Spake Zarathustra

To some of the readers it may seem that I stepped into woo-woo land again in the last chapter. All this talk about other-dimensional intelligences sounds like something out of *Star Wars*. But I have to ask the reader, just what did you expect from advanced cognitive awareness? What did you presume enlightenment was going to give you? Do you anticipate being one of those who has not disembarked from the plane in almost all of human history? What did you think it might lead you to, or did you ever really give it any deep consideration at all?

How is it easier to believe that aliens buzz the planet and abduct people than it is to accept the fact that other conscious entities are more easily accessible than the saucer jockeys? Naturally, in the realm of first cognition "reality", none of this is possible or even remotely real, right? These books have gone to great pains to reveal the reality perceived by the ego program, to show you the limited boundaries of what the ego demands reality to be. Do you think that those definitions are all there is to reality, that everything that exists must exist in 3D matter in order to be valid or remotely real?

These questions are not idle inquiries. These questions are highly relevant if you insist on proceeding into the second cognition. If you have gone through the process of advancing into the second cognition, or if you are still working on it, what are you going to do with it once you have found it? Ride on your laurels like all the so-called masters through the present day, stay stuck at the bottleneck of the hourglass and not venture forth into new territory? And if you plan to venture out to those new landscapes, what do you remotely think you are going to discover? What do you *expect* to discover? Do you anticipate discovering anything at all? The reader would be well advised to seriously consider all of these questions in regard to their spiritual quest.

If the reader doesn't ask themselves these questions and more, then you are not much different than a dog that chases every car that that goes by. What does that dog do when it finally catches a car? The dog has it in its teeth, now what is it going to do with it? I hope the reader can appreciate the analogy, for it is highly applicable. What do you intend to do with the second cognition when you reach it? We all get so involved in the chase, the pursuit of spiritual understanding, that we lose sight of what happens when we get there, if we even ponder that question to begin with.

As I have stated, spirit is extremely pragmatic. All these questions are pragmatic questions. All of these questions have answers, but one has to be ready to accept the answers. Are you really ready to accept the greater truths of the universe at large, or are you going to let your first cognition awareness continue to dictate to you what reality is and is not? This is exactly what I was writing about in the last chapter about the difficulty you will face as you start to fill out the bottom of that hourglass. All your definitions of reality are going to be challenged. How far you advance into second cognition understanding is totally predicated on your willingness to accept what you find there, and it will virtually all be limited by your willingness or unwillingness to accept what you discover there. If you stand in stark denial of everything spirit can show you, you will not progress too far into that new territory. Your own sense of denial and refusal to accept that reality will be the perceptual chains preventing any serious advancement. You can't continue to use the definitions of the first cognition to show you how to comprehend the second cognition forever. At some point you are going to have to expand your cognitive abilities to be more functional in that higher state of perceptual awareness.

In my last two books I made brief references to what Don Juan called *inorganic beings.* Carlos Castenada did a serious disservice to this truth by concocting imaginary realms inhabited by sinister geometrically shaped beings who tried to hijack him to their world. I am taking this section of the book to explain what *inorganic beings* are. Most readers are probably not going to be willing to accept what follows, but many readers are already involved with inorganic intelligences whether they are aware of it or not. What the reader chooses to believe or not is wholly on their shoulders. I am only providing information.

Before I get into further explanations on the matter I have to lay the groundwork of what an inorganic being is. Reincarnation is a fact, take it or leave it as you decide. Those who believe in a soul, whether they believe in reincarnation or not, hold some concept that they have a soul that may eventually go to some purported heaven or another. This soul, once it is outside of a human form is an inorganic being. It means that it is a consciousness that once inhabited a human form and is now a consciousness outside that form, without any organic form in matter - thus the term inorganic being.

Many people on this planet are already dealing with inorganic intelligences without having a clue as to who or with what they are dealing. In many cases, one's spirit guides are inorganic beings - intelligences that have lived in bodies made of matter at some point in their own soul's progression. Throughout human history these inorganic intelligences have been misinterpreted by those operating in the first cognition, defining them as dæmons as did the ancient Greeks, spirits or etheric beings.

Most of the modern channelers are under the sway of any one or a group of inorganic intelligences. It is not bad enough that these inorganic consciousnesses find it so easy to prey on humans operating from the misconception that communication with them is somehow divine or mystical, ego-driven humans craving the attention of being channelers are actually *inviting* these inorganic beings to manipulate their consciousness. The simple act of asking to be a channeler opens the door to all sorts of mischief to those who do not have an ounce of discernment to know the good guys from the bad guys out there, and like any human con man, they can appear benevolent but their true intentions are malevolent. There is no conscious entity operating with impeccability that will ever ask another to submit its mind to their will. Yet every channeler has to move over in their own head to let the channeled entity take over their consciousness in order to deliver their messages. This should be an automatic red flag to anyone purportedly delivering messages from anyone 'out there'.

Consciousness is not found in the brain. Consciousness is a form of energy. I am going to give you the best explanation I can in regard to consciousness as I have come to understand it. This explanation is by no means 100% accurate, and I have no doubt that there is substantially more to the equation that I have yet to become aware.

I am going to break it down into the three types of conscious beings with which I am currently familiar. Beings of pure consciousness, those who have never incarnated in matter form throughout their entire existence are what we refer to as the true etherics. Once an entity inhabits any form in matter, whether human or otherwise, and that consciousness leaves that form, they become inorganic beings. There is something about incarnation in matter that 'taints' etheric consciousness. This tainted carryover from matter is what created the inorganic consciousnesses. True etherics rarely have any interface with beings incarnated in matter, and for the most part, rarely if ever with an Earth human. So when you read the writers that refer to disembodied consciousnesses as etheric beings, they are actually talking about inorganic beings through their first cognition perceptual ignorance.

The channeled Tibetan masters of Madame Blavatsky, and Alice Bailey, as well as Aliester Crowley's *Aiwass* were all inorganic beings. Every entity that modern New Age channelers channel are inorganic beings, and since the time of Blavatsky and before, they all have an agenda, and it has nothing to do with human cognitive advancement.

I know all of this is a hard pill to swallow. I know for some it takes the author back into woo-woo land, but it doesn't make it untrue just because it doesn't fit into your current perception of reality. The fact is that Earth human consciousness is terribly easy to manipulate. No one wants to admit this fact, but the ease of manipulation comes from two major failings in human first cognition consciousness. The first failing is the belief in the mystical and supernatural. The second failing is a misplaced trust in inorganic voices sweet-talking us through dreams or other interactions. Both of these factors are but examples of first cognition gullibility and lack of understanding.

I recently picked up a book which I won't name to use as an example. The author of the book claimed to have had an entity contact her through repeated dream sequences. Being a first cognition pragmatic person who didn't really believe in such things, the author was naturally skeptical. Over time and through many dreams, the author came to trust the voice who spoke so sweetly and seemingly genuinely in her dreams. The author was given a set of tools that were purportedly designed to help people advance themselves. This routine of sweet-talking those lacking the discernment to know better is one of the easiest ways inorganic beings use to manipulate and deceive first cognition ego consciousnesses.

I paged through the book and it didn't take me long to discover that what these purportedly wonderful tools were, were nothing more than ego gratification tools, not that dissimilar from affirmations. They portrayed a process to soothe egos and make them feel they were somehow advancing themselves, all the while creating an energetic food supply for the inorganic being who transmitted the information.

This is going to get deep and hard to believe for most readers. Whether you accept it or not is wholly up to your own belief structure at this time. Everything in existence has to feed on something. Organic beings, like human beings and other beings in matter, feed off of other organic material in order to survive. In the realm of the inorganics or etherics, the food supply is comprised of certain types of energies, or energy emissions. There is energy created from belief systems. The more people who get roped into a belief structure, say a religion, who give up their personal energies in any form of worship or belief, are an energetic food supply for some being somewhere.

Let's take Theosophy as an example. Madame Blavatsky had her own inorganic 'master' who led her down the path to create Theosophy. Creating Theosophy itself was not much of a food supply to the inorganic being who called himself Koot Hoomi. In order for Theosophy to turn into an inorganic smorgasbord, it had to find followers who believed in it. Once the believers started multiplying and committing their energies into the belief system initiated by Koot Hoomi, all he had to do was sit back and feed off this energy to his inorganic heart's content.

I used just one example to make my point. You can take this principle and spread it across the board to Joseph Smith's purported angel Moroni, Aliester Crowley's *Aiwass*, and every inorganic entity masquerading themselves through virtually every channeler in the New Age arena as Jesus, the Mother Mary, members of the Galactic Federation of Light, the Siriun High Council, and good old Koot Hoomi himself who now has his name spelled Kuthumi. The inorganics, without any sense of impeccability, prey on human consciousness in this regard and they have throughout human history. They are simply predators of our consciousness.

Because our species has not developed any sense of spiritual discernment, we fall for the mystical twaddle presented by these predatory inorganic beings time after time. Earth humans are dangerously gullible in this regard. This is one of the major reasons I keep trying to impress on the reader the need to develop high discernment when dealing with invisible entities of any kind, no matter how *nice* they present themselves to be.

I realize that what I just presented is a pretty hard pill to swallow, but if you advance and you develop your own sense of discernment, you are going to discover these things for yourself. One doesn't have to be remotely close to the second cognition to play these games with the inorganics. The inorganics are ancient intelligences, they are not pikers by any stretch of the imagination. They have been manipulating incarnate consciousnesses throughout the universe as their food supply for untold eons. It is not just Earth humans who have been seduced by and fallen prey to the inorganic lures into their mystical mazes.

If you are one of those who has the communication ability to converse with your spirit guides, you most likely have the ability to communicate with other intelligent beings in the universe. I am presenting this section on the manipulations of the inorganic beings as a warning to you as you advance yourself in your quest for greater cognitive awareness. Regardless of whatever honey an inorganic being uses to lure you with, it will never stand up to serious scrutiny if one is diligent in questioning them.

The inorganic beings who prey on human consciousness, as Don Juan stated and with which I agree based on a lot of personal experience, are just as egotistical as first cognition humans. They all have a personal selfish agenda to use human consciousness as an energetic food supply. The best way to flush out one of these masqueraders is to ask them very pointed questions. The more questions one asks, the more pointed the questions you raise, the less these inorganic fraud artists have to say. Most of the time, if you ask them too much, they get testy in their responses or usually just go quiet. That is the best indicator I can give you to tell an inorganic manipulator from a genuine consciousness that has no personal ego agenda in deceiving you. The inorganic manipulators can't stand close scrutiny.

What I have just described, based on my own personal experiences, happens time and time again with the inorganic *players.* They can only prey on the gullible, uninformed, and those who lack discernment enough to even question them or their motives. This is why I emphasize to everyone I work with that you have to ask questions of your guides or any other intelligence you come into contact with. It is only through critical questioning that you learn to flush out the players.

As I noted above, these inorganic players are masqueraders, and they continue to get away with their nonsense because humans are so gullible. Too many people yearning for that mystical experience are simply asking to be abused by these inorganic beings. If you are one of those people who has communication with their guides, I advise you to set up passwords with them that only you and your guides know. This is one way to stop inorganic intruders from masquerading as your own personal spirit guides. Also, ask your guides if there is anything I just related that is untrue, and find out for yourself.

I offered some preliminary tools for advancing yourself vibrationally in *Demystifying the Mystical.* What was offered was only a primary tool to show certain readers that all this energy stuff is real. There is substantially more to the energetic equation than I revealed in that book, and over time it will be shared. The reason I bring up advancing one's vibrational signature is that many readers have been experiencing these energies for years. One of the key indicators for inorganic beings to target humans is when their energy signature starts to rise. The inorganics want human consciousness operating firmly in the first cognition operating at the lowest vibration possible, supplying their emotional energy to the fabricated belief systems developed by the inorganics. When the inorganics detect anyone starting to energetically elevate away from the lower 3D frequencies, that person becomes a target for the inorganics, in a very literal sense.

So, this brings us back to Nietzsche's quote at the chapter heading. In the first cognition, we are beleaguered with beliefs of all kinds and superstitions of all kinds. Many of these belief systems originated from outsides sources, a good percentage of the time originating from inorganic beings. Having explained everything I have in this chapter, it begs the question that Nietzsche asked, how many of you are *able* to believe?

Chapter 10

*"But wherever I found the living, there too I heard
the language of obedience. All that lives obeys.
And this is the second point: he who cannot obey
himself is commanded. Such is the nature of the
living."*

Friedrich Nietzsche - Thus Spake Zarathustra

I discovered much of what I related in the last chapter during my own period of transition before reaching the second cognition. The final understanding about the magnitude of the manipulation from the realm of the inorganic beings and learning the difference between an inorganic being and a true etheric only came about after I crossed that cognitive threshold and started my own explorations toward the bottom of the hourglass. Regardless of when I personally discovered this, it is information that doesn't hurt to have at your disposal for the sake of spiritual self-protection.

I said that as one starts to elevate their own vibrational capabilities that we become targets for the inorganics. In explaining this, we have to move into explanations about the workings of energy. Once again, for many readers, I am going into territory that most people are unfamiliar with, the exceptions being those who have either felt these energies, or are farting around with Reiki thinking they are doing something grand with the energy they manipulate.

I offered criticism on the practitioners of Reiki in *Demystifying the Mystical*. What follows is going to be a more in depth critique of Reiki as well as a deeper explanation about not only what it means to be targeted by inorganics, but how such targeting can impact us on the physical level.

Working with my partners over the years, we tried to track down the origin of so-called Reiki energy. Whatever the source of this energy is, it is not one of those naturally occurring energies of the cosmos. It is a fabricated energy. Ultimately, we discovered that Reiki energy was created by some group of inorganic intelligences designed to keep human energy levels operating at a very low frequency.

I explained how the inorganics prey on gullible and mostly ego-oriented personalities. Human beings can feel energy. Reiki generates a certain energy signature that many can feel and experience on a physical level. When one goes through what's called a Reiki attunement, they are basically setting themselves up as a conduit for this gang of inorganic beings who created Reiki energy and the belief system that originated from it through the Japanese inventor of Reiki, Dr. Mikao Usui. During his lifetime Dr. Usui personally trained 2,000 people. That's quite a foundation for establishing a belief structure for any inorganic being. From such humble beginnings, Reiki has become a global phenomenon, having practitioners all around the planet, and more clamoring by the day to be part of their ranks.

When a person receives their first attunement to Reiki, they are assigned a "Reiki Guide", who is supposed to guide them in how to best utilize the practice. So, let me digress for a moment and piss off every Reiki practitioner on the planet who reads this book.

People who first encounter Reiki are introduced to a form of energy that they can feel on their bodies. This energy is a "feel good" energy, and therefore seems to be innocuous. Because it makes people feel good, that feel good energy is the lure created by the inorganic beings to get more people to buy into their particular belief paradigm. Many people decide to pursue Reiki attunements based on their introduction to the feel good energy as 'patients' or subjects for 'healing'. The idea of becoming a Reiki healer or Master is very appealing to an ego, so there is no shortage of first cognition ego-oriented followers who just want to join in the fun and hopefully get the bragging rights of being a Reiki healer -- wooooh. It just sounds so *mystical*, doesn't it?

So we have the lure of the energy that gives Reiki a sense of validity, and then we have an ego that can't resist the bragging rights to elevate itself with the term healer or Master and learn how to throw these energies around. To use these energies gives an ego a platform to be *special* to the perception of other egos. The practitioners, followers and believers in the practice have now become unwitting agents for a group of inorganic beings that feed off their constructed belief system. All the energy that people put into giving Reiki credence become willing buffets for the inorganics who created the belief paradigm. And Reiki *must* be real, because we lowly humans can actually feel the energy! The emotions generated by the believers, not just the feel good belief itself, but the negative energies emitted to defend the belief system, are all ambrosia to the inorganic players - who are all laughing their inorganic behinds off at the gullible humans who buy into and support this belief system. This applies to every system of mystical or supernatural beliefs around the world.

Now, let's get to the Reiki Guides. Just who the hell are these purported guides and just where the hell do they come from? I'll bet you any money that not a single Reiki master ever bothered to ask that question. These ego-driven energetic Reiki saviors of mankind just accept this swill without question. I guess they all believe that some heavenly host of Reiki guides is lined up in a queue just waiting to serve mankind! I guarantee you that if any of these practitioners put these so-called guides under the microscope of critical questioning, as I suggested in the last chapter, every one of them would reveal themselves as inorganic manipulators. But you can't tell the practitioners that because their egos are so inflated with their presumed mastery to deny every word I wrote.

All creation is comprised of energy. Even the human form in matter is a form of compressed energies and multitudes of combined intelligences that make up our individual bodies. Our bodies are not a singular thing, we are each walking cities of combined intelligent particles of consciousness. If you have used cell talk as I presented it in *Demystifying the Mystical*, then you have to be aware that there is consciousness inside you down to the cellular level, and these conscious particles go down to the atomic and sub-atomic level. We are all walking communities of intelligence!

As I related in the last chapter, beings incarnated in matter are the food source of energetic inorganic beings. The inorganic beings are ancient and they are fully cognizant of how to manipulate energies. For a gang of them to come up with and create an energy called Reiki is child's play. You have to start advancing your consciousness to embrace such principles if you ever hope to advance into the second cognition. You have to expand your perceptual boundaries to accept that such things are not only possible but a very real aspect of creation.

You have to ask that if the inorganic beings can fabricate Reiki energy to lure people into their system of belief that feeds off of our emotional connection to the belief, why should we presume they can't manipulate other energies to repress our species as well? The fact is they can and they have throughout human history. When you start to elevate out of the lower ranges of human energetic vibrational energy, you become a threat to their food supply. Raising your vibration sets off a red flag with them that they are about to lose another candidate to their chicanery. When they notice one who is elevating themselves energetically they strike out in what I have come to call *hit energy*. I call being tagged with these energies as being *hit* because the inorganics throwing negative energy at you feels like someone hit you physically.

Make no mistake, this is not just all metaphysical or psychological woo-woo. If you get hit there are usually accompanying physical discomforts and sometimes physical marks left on the body after a hit. I am telling you this based not only on my own personal experience, but the experiences of a number of people I have worked with directly, and even those with whom I have had conversations over the years who have experienced hits and had no clue what they were until I explained about them. Many readers may have already experienced hits in the course of their own development and not known what they were.

The physical effects of hits can leave one with massive headaches, nausea or queasy stomachs that can last for days, feeling out of sorts or wonky for days with no real explanation for the feeling; cases of diarrhea, marks on the skin from a metaphysical attack, and in very bad cases, even broken bones.

From my own experience, to this day I still nurse a broken rib from a hit that happened while I was asleep on a waterbed. So make no mistake, metaphysical energetic hits have a physical price. One doesn't have to go looking for trouble. When your vibration starts to elevate beyond the level of the inorganic beings' food chain, they will come looking for you, and energetic hits are what they use to try and dissuade you from further vibrational advancement. Often times, hits come in as a powerful feeling of fear, an electric-like jolt all over your body not dissimilar to the jolt one gets from a heavy realization that creates cognitive dissonance. All of these actions are designed to dissuade the one advancing themselves energetically from continuing on their path.

The problem with the practice of Reiki is how people who practice it are so easily deceived into thinking it is something wholesome simply because their initial encounter with the energy makes them physically feel good. They never question whether something that feels good can be bad for you. They just accept it because it is a form of low vibration feel good energy and assume that there is no harm in using it. Deeper aspects of energetic manipulation will be covered in volume 5 of this series when my wife and spiritual partner shares her own personal experiences with energy in *The Energy Experience: Energy Work for the Second Cognition.*

It doesn't take a very high frequency energy to convince low vibrational first cognition humans that the energy is real. The greatest problem lies in their lack of critical questioning into the matter. The ego gets all wrapped up in the mystical applications and feels that they are something special if they can learn to do the same thing. The harmful aspect of Reiki is only presented when an individual who has reached an elevated vibratory state that goes beyond Reiki submits themselves to Reiki energy. I know I covered some of this in *Demystifying the Mystical*, but it doesn't hurt to reiterate it here. It is *important* information.

Reiki energy is specifically designed to keep humans operating solely at the bandwidths that the inorganic beings feed from. If one has elevated their vibration somewhat beyond this range and submits to a Reiki session, the lower vibrational Reiki energy causes a state of physical imbalance, headaches and nausea. The effects are not permanent, but they can leave one feeling out of sorts for days. To all the Reiki practitioners out there, if you can set your glorified egos aside, I challenge you to question your so-called Reiki guides and see if they don't try to misdirect you, get testy with your critical questions or simply go quiet when the questions get too hard. That is all the proof you need to validate to yourself what I just wrote.

When one learns Reiki, they have to learn the symbols that Dr. Usui created when he manufactured the practice. Even if one doesn't trace the symbols in the air, most Reiki masters are required to learn the symbols as part of receiving becoming a reiki healer. By following this practice, just as Nietzsche noted in the chapter header, you are simply obeying the instructions of others. You are taking all of this crap on faith. You are not obeying yourself as spiritual self-mastery requires. You are simply obedient to the designs of others, in this case inorganic intelligences.

This obedience is not just restricted to Reiki practices. Every belief system has its rules to follow. If you are following someone else's rules, you are simply obedient. You are obeying others, not yourself. The entire first cognition system is predicated on obedience in one form or another, if you think about it. Surviving and defending the first cognition is a form of unwitting obedience to the system.

Aliester Crowley had his own inorganic guide in the entity *Aiwass,* who later claimed to be Horus. Just as the Reiki practitioners buy into their own form of inorganic manipulation, the followers of Crowley - the Thelemites - are just another food supply for a group of inorganics with their own agenda. The same can be said of the New Age and all the channelers who are nothing more than conduits to inorganic beings pumping down their doctrinal swill for the consumption of the masses of gullible and non-discerning ego personalities operating in the first cognition with a craving for the supernatural. The whole love and light doctrine is manufactured by these inorganic beings.

Epiphanies from Angels, where the receiver claims to feel the 'love of God', are nothing more than inorganic beings throwing down feel good energy to some human who wants to experience the supernatural or mystical. When a believer begs and pleads for some kind of sign, you can bet there is some inorganic player waiting in the wings to satisfy that yearning with some kind of perceived *holy* message and a dose of feel good energy to convince the pleader that it was a divine supernatural experience - a miracle! So long as people remain uninformed about such entities as the inorganic beings and their practices and tactics, the lunacy and deception will continue.

Chapter 11

"False values and delusive words: these are the worst monsters for mortals -- calamity sleeps and waits long in them."

Friedrich Nietzsche -- Thus Spake Zarathustra

This series of books is meant as an exposé of the failings of human consciousness when we are operating strictly in the first cognition. It is a world of perceptual illusion controlled and driven by words and definitions. The values humanity professes to adhere to in that cognition are open to interpretation and are often altered depending on which institution is in control at any give time in history. It is my desire that through the presentation of information I am providing, that the reader can see exactly what Nietzsche is referring to with the quote for this chapter.

If we are not misguided by people in power, we are open to being misguided by other more ancient intelligences that prey on our consciousnesses as illustrated in the last two chapters. The meanings of words often change over time, so words are always delusive when it comes to manipulating the minds of ego-driven, fearful first cognition humans. The question every reader has to ask themselves is how long do they intend to be deluded by the words and perceptual illusions of the first cognition consciousness?

My books are hard-hitting. I realize that I am throwing decades worth of personal investigations at you in a very short format. In one sense, I am not giving you the luxury of time to find out many of these things on your own, but many of the things I am relating have either not yet been discovered or related by others. I know that some readers have been doing their own investigations into some of these matters for probably as many years as I did. A lot of the readers are looking into certain aspects of globalist political control, and many have a pretty good idea about the crap going on in the world. Even reading the comments sections of the mainstream news threads is showing that many people are starting to pull themselves out of the illusions of political manipulation. As stated in a previous chapter, the soil is thin, but mighty trees may yet grow from it.

In all honesty, I do not have high expectations for humanity in general at this point of our history. There are too many lies and fictions hiding the truth from all of us. When I write about finding the truth, I neglected to emphasize that we also have to find the lies. Not only do we have to find the lies, we have to admit that we believed the lies for so many years. The vast majority of people are completely unwilling to challenge their own perceptual belief systems because accepting the truth in the alternative is just downright frightening. This fear controls all their minds.

The internet is replete with information, but unfortunately, many people believe that it is a better source of truth than mainstream outlets. Many have not yet realized that there is just as much disinformation on the internet as elsewhere. One thing that troubles me is how readily so many buy into conspiracy theories without doing the real legwork required to really uncover facts which in many cases expose the lies of the conspiracy theory being hawked. One of the most pernicious myths is the one about the Illuminati. The alleged Illuminati is the boogey man of first cognition conspiracy flag wavers. They put the claim of the existence of the Illuminati at the feet of Adam Weishaupt predicated on a letter found on a dead, lightning struck messenger in 1784. Weishaupt did organize a spy network which he named the Order of the Illuminati. To read modern Illuminati propaganda, the Illuminati goes back thousands of years to ancient Egypt.

Much of the Illuminati propaganda is linked to the Freemasons, because Weishaupt was a Mason. Weishaupt's Order of the Illuminati was banned as seditious by the German government, yet the Illuminati mythology and the threat of a global Illuminati takeover keeps many first cognition egos enthralled and fearful to this day. Make no mistake, there are those who have an agenda for global societal control, but they are not the so-called Illuminati. The Illuminati is a paper tiger used to make the uninformed fear a non-existent boogey man. There are agents of disinformation, well known shock jocks who shall remain unnamed, who daily pump out this Illuminati swill to a gullible and fearful public. It is all just another form of first cognition mind control through fear.

During my years of investigating into many areas of research, I have to honestly admit that there was a time I bought into a lot of that swill myself. But the deeper I investigated, I finally came to see all of that type of disinformation is nothing more than another fear mechanism to control the masses. If you are one who happens to still believe in a lot of that hype, you would be wise to recognize it for the manipulation of your consciousness that it is and move past it. Get past the fear being hyped and discover the deeper truths hidden behind the propaganda of fear.

In order to understand the manipulation from all quarters against first cognition humans, you will find that all alleged sides play against the middle. We have the illusion of the left being different than the right, but no matter which party is in power, no matter the rhetoric they use, it is a continual erosion of personal freedoms. We have the illusion of one religion being different from another. Doctrinally speaking that may be true, but the purported differences always lead to the same conclusion where first cognition manipulation is concerned. It is one group of people making other people obey their rules.

Your mission in moving to the second cognition is to outgrow all such forms of manipulation of your own consciousness. If you develop and maintain your own spiritual impeccability you will find that you need no rules, values, morals or laws devised by first cognition humans to dictate to you what is right for your spirit self. Valid information is publicly available as to who the worst perpetrators seeking global control are. I can tell you that there is not one singular dynamic entity controlling these things. There are a number of different factions involved, and some of them are very ancient. The idea for world domination is not new. Alexander the Great and many other first cognition humans have had that idea over the centuries and tried to implement it.

I am not going into the specific details of just who these varied factions are because it is too lengthy to address, and basically you need to do your own homework on the subject. There is no shortage of valid information available if you can develop the ears to hear the message and dig it out for yourself. I can't be expected to give you everything you want to know. I'm throwing enough cognitively disruptive information at you as it is.

I first brought up Leon Festinger's *A Theory of Cognitive Dissonance* in my book, *Willful Evolution*. Although Festinger was writing his theory from strictly a first cognition viewpoint, many of his observations are even more cogent when one considers the second cognition. He makes note of the fact that when a cognitive definition of reality is based on social acceptance, where the majority of people believe in an accepted reality, then the chances of altering that cognition are virtually non-existent. This is exactly where we find ourselves today in discussing the second cognition and why the vast majority of people functioning in the first cognition will not accept the possibility of its existence, let alone inquire into it. The social constraints of all human societies serve as a pressure point to keep people firmly rooted within the boundaries of the first cognition.

Every group subset of the first cognition serves as its own agent of enforcement for their particular projected belief structures, and they are all contained within and governed by the overall first cognition definition of reality. Many of you may have already experienced the discomfort of those rigidly bound in the first cognition protesting and ridiculing what you are trying to achieve. This pressure is particularly hard to deal with when it comes from friends, family and peer groups. This cognitive resistance is part of the nature of the protectors of the ego reality. If you have not yet experienced this type of cognitive resistance, sooner or later you will.

When people choose to deride you or your ideas, they are exhibiting what Festinger called behavioral cognitive responses. These negative responses are the pressure from the herd to comply with the orders and commands of the herd, to obey what the herd mentality mandates reality to be. The behavioral responses to protecting their own cognition are their negative denigrating remarks and insults, all designed to make you compliant to the demands of their cognitive reality. It is a form of negative reinforcement, not much unlike shame programming we are all subjected to during our lives.

Any time an ego can make another ego feel insecure, either of themselves or their beliefs, tactics for negative reinforcement eventually come into play. Negative reinforcement and ostracization are the weapons the herd uses to generate compliance with its operating rules under the first cognition. The herd feels that if it isolates the offender that the herd will be protected from its poisonous influences. The practice of excommunication used by the Catholic Church was a form of negative reinforcement to control the masses of its followers for centuries. The fear of not being buried in hallowed ground was another such tool used to insure group compliance through threat.

You are free to pick your own brand of group reinforcement to see this example in your own life. It doesn't matter exactly which pressure tool is used against you, someone in the herd will always try to find a way to pressure you to their point of view and bring you back into the fold of the first cognition. If you intend to succeed on your journey into the second cognition, you are going to have to have exceptional strength of spirit to not succumb to such external pressures. It is not an easy journey for anyone. I paid my dues in that regard. I had long-time friends who got frightened of me and fell away even before I reached the level of second cognition awareness. They couldn't deal with the truths I was discovering and sharing with them. It undermined their whole worldview so much that avoiding me and ending friendship was the only way they felt they could preserve their own perceptual reality.

This is one of the major reasons this path is not for everyone. Most do not have the psychological courage to withstand the strain the path can often present. As I have repeatedly stated, it takes profound courage to do this thing and ultimately achieve success. The vast majority want to maintain their comfortable perceptual world and not have to do anything more than function as a cog in the first cognition machine. This is not recriminations against their spirit self, because most of them are not in touch with that inner guide in the least. It is, however, a recrimination against the ego programming that controls their lives.

Chapter 12

"He who has grown wise concerning old origins,
behold, he will at last seek springs of the future
and new origins ---
O my brothers, it will not be long before *new
peoples* shall arise and new springs rush down
into new depths."

Friedrich Nietzsche - Thus Spake Zarathustra

If you are reading this material and benefiting from the information I am sharing, then there is every chance that you are one of the *new peoples* Nietzsche referenced. You have to face the truth about the old origins of where the first cognition has been firmly lodged since *homo sapiens sapiens* arrived late on the stage of the evolution of the universe. We have to stop looking backward to define ourselves as a species. It is time we learned the lessons of all those things past and turn our eyes toward a different future. It is time we advance from the shallow world of ego and become those rushing springs that have a depth the ego can never know. Do you have it in you?

Looking at the condition of the world, which seems to be getting more and more out of control every day, it is very hard to not get discouraged and even frightened. This is one reason that spiritual detachment is so important. At one time I watched world events and worried about everything that was happening around me. I worried and fretted, allowing my ego to taunt me with fatalistic 'what if' games for most of my life. During my period of transition, I learned to develop the spiritual detachment that allowed me to observe how the world was going down the trash around me without having the emotional investment my own ego once insisted I had to maintain in its world. Once I attained this detachment, the emotional concerns of my former ego were shown to be needless worry most of the time.

The world of the first cognition is going to be the way those trapped in it make it to be. I could spend my life fretting over all the ills in the world and have sleepless nights like I did for many years, concerned whether someone was going to push the big red button or not. Spiritual detachment gave me the distance to view all the happenings in the first cognition without becoming emotionally upset at the continued arrogance and stupidity of a world run by egos hopelessly lost in their perceptual illusions. Yes, I have certain concerns about the stupidity and horror going on in the world, but I also realize there is nothing I can personally do, other than writing these books, to alter either their cognitive perception or their cognitive behavior.

I had to decide what was more important in my own life, worrying all the time about politics, religion, racial strife and the constant threat of warfare that hangs over every head on the planet, or should my focus be on development of my own consciousness. You already know the choice that I made. The question is if you have the strength to go down that road to cognitive freedom or not.

I offered the process of how to ask for energy downloads from our sun, Ra, in *Demystifying the Mystical*. I also suggested asking for energetic downloads from the planets in our local solar system. Gaining spiritual detachment is not an easy thing to do, especially when we are still roped into ego habits. We have all developed the group mentality of feeling we have to care about things in the first cognition herd mentality. One of the greatest questions that egos ask is, "Don't you care?" It is this inherent necessity that the ego needs for everyone to care about something that is hard to overcome on the road to gaining detachment. If one becomes emotionally detached, they won't care any more (at least not in the same emotional sense), and that idea on its own is enough to scare the daylights out of any ego. This is the primary reason so many get off their paths. They want to maintain the self-image of who their egos say they are and therefore refuse to change.

Having said that, more explanation is necessary for your complete understanding about spiritual detachment. What we think of as caring in the first cognition is all about ego-driven emotions. You see, an ego can't imagine someone caring without exhibiting the accompanying emotion that goes along with caring in the ego's perception. How many times have you been asked, "Don't you *care* about me?" Just this one simple question expresses exactly what I am trying to relate about egos needing the emotional investment that is associated with the idea of caring.

I care about a lot of things that are happening around the world, but I have no longer have an emotional reactive need attached to that caring. I feel no personal requirement to care about any ego's emotional demands or needs. It doesn't mean I can't care. It simply means I will not invest myself emotionally over what I care about the same way those operating in ego require that emotional commitment from themselves and others. One can easily care about things without the emotional connection. This is what detachment is about; to be able to maintain your passions, caring, love and other feelings without having the emotions serving as the reactive generator to the feelings. One can feel, in a sensory capacity, without having the emotional sensations running the show. Because the ego is so controlling through its necessity for emotional enrichment and validation, it can't conceive of feelings without reactionary emotions being attached.

The reason I brought up the process of asking for downloads is this. Every star or constellation provides certain energies when asked, and when one is ready to receive them vibrationally. The energy that is best to start developing your own level of detachment comes from the constellation Draco. Asking for a download from Draco will provide you with the energetic framework on which you can build your own sense of detachment. As you receive the download, you will feel and totally understand detachment. Admittedly, this detachment energy may be quite disconcerting to you because it may seem to run counter to how you have emotionally acted all your life, but the energy itself is not unpleasant and is generally accessible even if your own personal vibration has not yet elevated that high.

If you do choose to ask for this download, rest assured that the detachment you may feel while the energy download is in progress, which can feel quite pronounced, will even out after the download completes. Using Draco energy is one of what I consider to be valid *shortcuts* in this process. Using the download option does not undercut the other things you have to accomplish for yourself, but having that sense of detachment can help as you go through the whittling down process of your first cognition perceptual beliefs. The Draco energy provides a foundation upon which you can continue to build your own sense of detachment.

I realize there are some readers who are going to be skeptical and choose to disbelieve what I just related and they will not even try to do what I suggest for a multitude of varying personal reasons. Whether any reader chooses to use this tool or not is totally up to their own discretion. Those who do will see the benefits from the process. Those who don't, won't. You are each responsible for any advantage you gain from these writings and the tools provided herein. I have no concern whether you believe or disbelieve. I know it works and all those I have worked with know it works. The only way any reader is going to find out whether it works or not is to try it. You are in charge of yourself.

Now I have to address all this foolishness being promoted in New Age and certain conspiracy circles about shape-shifting reptiles from Draco. I told you how the inorganic beings can manipulate our consciousness. The inorganic beings feed on our emotional energy output. The last thing they want to see their human energetic food source do is stop generating high-level emotionally-fluctuating energies. The inorganic players know that if we humans ever learn to tap into the detachment energy provided by Draco through the download process I just described, the inorganics will eventually starve when our rampant first cognition emotional energies no longer feed them.

From the standpoint of an inorganic player, how would you try to stop your human food source from tapping into that detachment energy? Maybe fabricate stories about shape-shifting reptiles to scare people away from Draco energy entirely? Well, I'm here to tell you folks, that's exactly what they have done, and the people most likely to tap into that energy are the ones targeted for this type of propagandized fear-generating disinformation. All one has to do is mention Draco to a New Ager or conspiracy theorist, and the fear cranks up and the good old reliable shape-shifting lizard appears in the conversation in an instant. The propagandized programming has taken so well that probably many readers of this book set it down in horror just at my mention of Draco. They will probably not even read as far as this explanation before they throw the book across the room scared to death from me just mentioning Draco, thinking they will somehow be infected by alien shape-shifting reptiles by simply reading the word Draco presented in a positive light.

When I make these assertions, they are based on numerous personal experiences watching people's reactions from my simply mentioning Draco. The fear programming is so deeply embedded that you can't convince them otherwise. The shape-shifting lizards from Draco is nothing more than the old 'aliens going to eat your face' scare tactic wrapped in a new package. I share these personal experiences to show you just how easy humans in the first cognition are to manipulate through any type of fear propaganda, and also to illustrate how such fear based in nonsense controls people. You have to be strong enough to see through and transcend this type of programming if you want to be successful in your journey. If not, the malarkey will continue to control your mind.

Chapter 13

"Better, truly, to live among hermits and goatherds than with our gilded, false, painted mob -- though it call itself 'good society'."

Friedrich Nietzsche - Thus Spake Zarathustra

I was recently talking to a close friend about the second cognition, and he expressed the process being similar to a birthing, but that one is stuck in the birth canal for years before they emerge out the other side. I thought this was a very cogent comparison due to the fact that this whole process *is* a form of birthing. You are working to be born again as a self-created, fully responsible independent consciousness. This entire concept of being born again is what the man we know as Jesus was referring to when he used that term to those he taught, and nothing more. Sadly, the first cognition misinterpreters of his message created a bunch of supernatural swill and spawned a new religion that has bloodily haunted the world for almost 2,000 years. We can only wonder how different the world might be if his message had been truly understood and adopted by mankind as a whole, rather than being bastardized and corrupted into false religious dogma.

Nietzsche saw the same fault in the created religions, although he had great respect for the teacher whose teachings were corrupted as a basis to start Christianity. The same thing happened with the teachings of Siddhartha Guatama - Buddha. We find ourselves in a world today rife with first cognition misinterpretations about virtually all teachings of spirit. Each of the spiritual schools teach certain kernels of the truth, but these truths are only partially revealed and have been patently misunderstood throughout the ages because the truths are revealed in riddles - or what appear to be riddles from the limited interpretive system of the first cognition. One only has to look at the spiritual and religious doctrines that survive and thrive around the world in order to see this.

From the standpoint of their own personal and group egos, they are all good people, good societies. The saying at the chapter heading encapsulates what Nietzsche tried to relate about the falsity of the entire cognitive system of the ego. Religions, science, academia, politics and everything else you can point to in the first cognition shows these perceptual failings if one is wise enough to see them. Coming to term with this grandiose cognitive illusion is a hard thing to do. It made me uncomfortable over the years as I gained more insight into the whole gross network of false perceptions that the first cognition mentality breeds. It is not going to be any easier for any reader to come to terms with this than I did, so be advised that this is yet another part of this self-birthing that one must grow through to advance their own conscious awareness into the second cognition.

Being intellectually aware of and accepting all of this is not the same as understanding it all from a higher perceptual perspective, but it is a necessary start. There is a vast difference in reading such things as revealed in this series of books and saying, "Yeah, I can believe that," and moving into the cognitive realm of *knowing* it on a deep level of heightened conscious awareness. It is this type of knowing where the Greek word *gnosis* has any real meaning. Knowledge in the sense of being able to recite cataloged and inventoried facts is not *gnosis*, it is simply thinking you know, when in actuality you truly *know* knowing.

The friend I referenced who shared his insight into this process being a long birthing process achieved his own shift of consciousness walking a path that did not include us comparing notes along the way to get there. He figured it out for himself, and only recently have we compared notes on the second cognition after walking our separate roads to get to the same place after almost two decades of friendship. We live far apart and have personally met on only two occasions, both of them many years ago, Much of what I am sharing in this books he did not discover (such as the information about the inorganic beings and the energy downloads), but he struggled and pushed his own envelope as I did to reach that next level of cognitive awareness.

I recently made acquaintance with another person in another country who, through their own individual process had also reached past the bottleneck of the hourglass to get firmly established in the second cognition. We compared notes and now we share our individual perceptual journeys together as friends who have a more serious basis for friendship than the first cognition can ever beget. I know there are others out there, thousands, potentially millions who are also well on the way into that greater realm of cognitive understanding, but who lack the information presented in these books to explain things to them in a more cogent manner than anything currently in the spiritual marketplace anywhere in the world. It is to these people who are in a serious period of cognitive transition that I write these words of explanation and encouragement. I want each and every one of you to know you are not alone in your personal quest for understanding. You are not alone, despite the turmoil and resistance you receive from those firmly rooted in the first cognition who seem to oppose what you are doing at every turn.

I am not aiming these writings at those who are deeply entrenched in the first cognition, who can only cast aspersions on those they not only can't understand, but don't want to understand. This is why the books have served as a weeding out process for those who choose to weed themselves out of the equation because they do not yet have, nor may ever have the will to power to do this thing in this lifetime. The message is aimed for those who can get it, for those who will do the work required to advance themselves. Only the individual reader can decide if the message is for you.

From my own experience, I clawed around and dug into information for years trying to unravel the so-called mysteries of spirit. Admittedly, I did not fall for name-dropping, seminar attending variety in my pursuits, but I spent a lot of money on books doing my research over the years. I probably spent a few thousand dollars on research materials of all kinds, up to and including high dollar college level course books in translated ancient texts in order to find what I was seeking. I have little doubt that many reading these words have also spent a lot of time, if not a lot of money, searching out these same answers. If you are still trying to get to the bottom of all this spiritual understanding, then you are part of the audience to whom I address these writings. If, however, you find that you have found your spiritual niche and are content to stay where you are and defend your beliefs in the face of opposing perspectives, then you are not who this series is written to reach. If you are merely a defender, you are a lost cause until you choose to move yourself forward. If you can't do that, you will remain stuck where you are, firmly rooted as an *agent* of the first cognition in the same sense of the agents in *The Matrix* films.

As a general rule, you are not going to find those who are in the process of advancing themselves in the first cognition arenas of group-think. They are most likely already hermits because they are tired of beating their heads against the unmoving walls of first cognition ignorance posing as knowledge. They become hermits out of necessity as a form of preservation of their own sanity in an insane world. These hermits have run the gamut of teachings out there and found all of them insufficient, that the teachings only go so far and then quit. It doesn't matter which religious, spiritual, mystical or esoteric schools of thought we have researched, we always come up with zip at the end of the day. We find ourselves surrounded with guessers and speculators about the unknown, who mostly don't have any real desire to progress into that unknown, but merely want it *explained* in a manner their first cognition abilities can accept.

You do not have to be fully progressed into the second cognition to start to understand these things if you are serious on your path. The realizations I am sharing with you are part of that transition period we all have to face and grow through. You could call it the growing pains of your own spirit self in this self-birthing process to be born again into a new system of cognitive awareness. None of these explanations are designed to project any kind of elitist arrogant mentality, regardless of whether one's first cognition interpretive powers are still highly active or not. This is a psychologically painful process, and I have spared no amount of words to express that. If you are already experiencing these growing pains, rest assured that they will pass in time if you stay the course, but the transition period is no cakewalk for anyone. Many people can't deal with this process and find some comfortable group setting in which they can present themselves as somehow knowledgeable on things they truly lack understanding, or they fall back into the pattern of first cognition spiritual dabblers. I have seen no shortage of both kinds of people on every spiritual website out there.

I have seen the pleaders and the whiners begging to know about spirit, but when you try to give them what they claim they want to know, they want to disagree because their ideas conflict with the hard truth of the spirit path. On one hand they beg to know, yet on the other hand, they presume they already know, so they shut their ears and learn nothing and keep seeking someone who will validate their own perceptual illusions - a like-minded person. You will often encounter the flip explanation that "Everyone has their own path," as justification for not wanting to hear the truth. Yes, everyone has to walk this path on their own, but using that excuse to sidestep the truth in favor of letting your ego defend its beliefs is not the same thing. It is no different that religionists copping out by saying that "God works in mysterious ways." It is simply an ego avoiding what it refuses to acknowledge.

The other types are the arrogant egos who have spent years memorizing and theorizing on Kabala or the teachings of Crowley, the Masons, the Neo-Pagans, Wicca, the Rosicrucian's and the Theosophists. Every bit of this is useless ego-inflating swill just as much as claiming to be some kind of spiritual Master of any stripe is. Their profound 'understanding' is nothing more than informational hogwash that inflates their own egos into believing they know things about which they have no clue.

I am not going to resort to naming names, because if the reader has been seeking information for any length of time at all, they have encountered the same names over and over again - the presenters of information - the pulpit pounders of the conspiracy and how their own specific brand of spirituality can guide the followers out of the maze of misunderstanding. If you do any kind of unbiased research on these people, you will find that most of them are associated with the Blavatsky/Bailey schools of Theosophy. Their video presentations and seminars are rife with esoteric symbolism and they are each chockfull of information about what these symbols *really* mean, according to their own brand of doctrinal swill.

I have explained in this series about a specific political agenda behind a goodly percentage of the modern New Age belief systems. What you will find with many of these so-called New Age conspiracy pulpit pounders is a heavy reliance on Jewish mystical traditions, often referring to Cabbalistic teachings and using all sorts of explanations to the purported Tree of Life within that tradition. Along with this you find support of Jewish belief systems of the Old Testament, also found heavily utilized in Masonic symbolism, and you will find purported links to the ancient Egyptians and ultimately back to Atlantis or Lemuria.

All of this swill seems to be cut from the same piece of cloth, and the true seeker of their own cognitive advancement has to wonder why such emphasis is put on all this symbolism and ancient mystical traditions when not an ounce of it is required knowledge to understand what you are trying to achieve. You have to ask, what is the real agenda in peddling all this claptrap and who ultimately benefits if the gullible and ignorant masses dedicate themselves to understanding this nonsense? In all honesty, have I provided anything in this material that remotely says that any of that crap is valid or necessary? Granted, I have shared new and possibly challenging concepts in these books, but you don't see me emphasizing any knowledge that so-called experts in the esoteric traditions say you need in order to understand to become spiritually aware. They claim to have wisdom and expertise in these matters because they have studied the script for years, but where is any of that swill necessary given what I have explained to the reader by now?

In many respects, it is like an old Chinese story about a man who got his hands on the wisdom teachings of every master that he could find. He studied all these materials until he had all knowledge about them that any man could. One day, the kingdom in which he lived was under attack, and he convinced his king that he had read all of the ancient wisdom books and had the knowledge to defeat the invader. Needless to say, they were conquered. The point of this story is to illustrate that one may have all the knowledge in the world and still not understand anything. The man's knowledge was useless without the understanding to apply it. This is the same trap that all these spiritualist cum conspiracy theorists fall into. They possess much knowledge about the subjects they teach people, but they have zero understanding about what they claim to know. With the material presented in this series of books in hand, you have more knowledge that can lead to understanding than all of the so-called ancient mystical or esoteric traditions can ever teach you. Understanding comes in applying knowledge, not in simply possessing dead information and calling it knowledge.

Chapter 14

"Overcome these masters of today, O my brothers
- these little people: *they* are the Übermensche's
greatest danger!"

Friedrich Nietzsche - Thus Spake Zarathustra

I have covered this whole issue of mastery in the last few chapters. Most of that focus has been on the spiritual arena, but we can't neglect all the other purported masters - those who possess Master's Degrees in all the varied fields of scientific and academic endeavors. As I have stated repeatedly throughout this book, I am disparaging no one's intelligence or level of achievements in their specific fields of endeavor. I am, however, challenging the arrogance of the ego in the first cognition that comes with any title of Master no matter where it is found and utilized as a measure of one's ego success. As stated previously, any time the term Master is used, it automatically brings with it the idea of a subservient or slave to the Master, an underling.

Within the trades fields I understand the Master Electrician, the Master Mason as a title for expertise in practices. I also understand Master's degrees in becoming doctors, for even that is a highly skilled level of experiential tradesmanship. But when you find Master's degrees in subjects such as Philosophy, what is their claim to tradesmanship, that they can play a better game of "what if" than their cohorts in the same practice of speculation? Ah, but they are Masters of their field, and they will not hesitate to tell you all about it! Even with all of this classification of mastery, the inherent problem in all of it is how an ego uses such titles to elevate and inflate itself. It is the bragging rights and the accompanying arrogance that shows any type of so-called mastery for what it is, if the title of Master is tossed about by an ego to place itself on a pedestal over others. The pretentious bravado and bluster of a full fledged first cognition ego Master is utterly unbearable to those who surround them. But such a claim of presumed mastery, as with Tibetan monks of the Buddhist tradition, is equally unbearable with their smirks of wisdom as they entice their students in their own form of the mastery game.

It is not in mastering a trade or skill that one in the second cognition can't recognize and accept. It is the pretentious bluster, the smarmy sense of superiority all these 'masters' exhibit that shows that they are not really very highly advanced cognitive beings, no matter how intelligent they are, nor how presumably wise they present themselves to be.

All forms of mastery in all these regards are the greatest threat to the overman because they are lures to keep oneself in the first cognition. As I have gone to great lengths to illustrate, we can see how pursuing mastery of any kind serves to entice one to stay in the first cognition, but in a presumably elevated position over the lowly others who are not masters. It is a seducer to the path to cognitive advancement. This is why it is the greatest danger to one on the path, because of its powerful seductiveness. It is also the acclaimed masters who are going to lodge the most powerful criticisms in order to protect their perceptual turf. Within the realm of the first cognition, the masters are the *authorities* that everyone listens to when they speak.

I don't claim mastery in any of the things I am explaining to the reader. I am on a path of continual development through which I think no one can truly become a master. Using the term mastery denotes an end, a specified goal of attainment. If you are on this path thinking that you are ever going to get rewarded with some kind of mastery in the process, you are only deceiving yourself. The more you venture into the second cognition, the more you discover that what you learn is inconsequential in the grand scheme of things. This game within all creation is so pregnant with potential, no consciousness in existence has mastered it, nor do I think any sentient being ever will because it is a creational process that is ever continuing and ever expanding.

My friend who shared the observation about the birthing process also made another observation in our last conversation that I thought was rather insightful. Humans operating in the first cognition seem to be stuck in a paradigm where they fear endings, and they fear things that are unending and unknown even more. We fear endings in relationships, endings in jobs (especially if it is unexpected), ending of life, as just three prime examples. As for the never ending or the unknown, that fear arises from a finite consciousness that can't even remotely imagine such a thing as infinity. Oh sure, they can profess living for eternity in heaven with their god, but few of them have deeply contemplated what eternity or infinity actually is. It's one thing to say the soul lives forever, but entirely something else to ponder what the hell your soul is supposed to do when you have eternity to work it out.

These are not philosophical observations designed to screw with your head. I invite the reader to try to move out of the finite thinking of the first cognition, and think about a level of consciousness that is not finite, that has no ending, that has eternity to create itself and re-create itself over and over into ever-expanding horizons of potential conscious advancement. Imagine, if you can, a vista for potential that is only limited by the cognitive perception of your eternal spirit self. Such a concept scares the snot out of most people. The move into the second cognition is only the first step on this road to infinity. At every point of your advancement you will master certain skills of perception, but you will not be a master in the sense that the first cognition perceives mastery. The first cognition interpretation of Master denotes an ending, a pinnacle to something. The more deeply you navigate into the second cognition, the more you can perceive that there is no pinnacle. There is only an ever-progressing *more*.

If you can become excited about this ever-unfolding journey of discovery, then you are one who will advance in the second cognition and beyond. If you fear this idea, then your own fear will handicap you on this journey. If you are only seeking first cognition mastery, you have already failed your spirit self.

An inherent danger to one on the path of the second cognition is the puffed up opinions and criticisms of these so-called little people of knowledge called Masters that will work tirelessly to ridicule you in hope of keeping you subservient to their presumed mastery in the first cognition reality. The all-knowledgeable masters at every turn will scorn your efforts, and if you buy into any of their presumptuous Master's ego pomposity, you will be lost. If you submit and agree that they are your masters, then you will ever be the slave to their inflated ego perceptions of themselves and their first cognition ideas. They can only remains Masters to those who give their allegiance and subservience to their proclaimed mastery. One can't become the master of one's spirit self if they bow to the presumed ego mastery of another. No one can be the authority of the direction of your own spirit except you. In that regard, you have no masters. The only thing you have to master is discovering who you really are beneath the programmed layers of your own ego.

Chapter 15

*"It is difficult to live among men, because it is so
hard to be silent."*

Friedrich Nietzsche - Thus Spake Zarathustra

There is no known teacher about advanced conscious
awareness that has remained silent. Each of them has seen the
fruitlessness and folly of the first cognition awareness. Each of
them was compelled, or felt a spiritual *push* to try and inform
people about the errors of the ways of the first cognition. Most of
these teachers were received with scorn, ridicule and often
downright hatred by the controllers of the masses. The protectors
of the domain of the first cognition have ever been the swine that
Jesus taught to not cast pearls of wisdom before because they are
liable to trample you under their feet, turn against you and tear
you apart. Every teacher met with scorn in one form or another
from limited first cognition ignorance at all levels.

Jesus went up against the Pharisees, Buddha challenged
Brahmanism, Nietzsche challenged all religions - particularly
Christianity, and also challenged the elite and educated, as did
Jesus. The more one looks into these people the more they can

see the similarity of messages they tried to teach, and the more one can see how each one of them was persecuted by the powers of their times for telling the truth that those in the first cognition refused to hear. Every one of them was trampled under the feet of first cognition swine for professing the same truth. I have no doubt that modern day swine would also love to trample this author under their feet and tear me apart for sharing the same critical message in a different form - for tearing down the walls of their belief structure. I invite the reader to read Jesus' Sermon on the Mount in light of the revelations shared in these books. I ask that you remove all the additional glosses about God and religion from his sayings, and see if you can see that his message was exactly the same message shared by Nietzsche, Buddha and this author. Don Juan was so circumspect in only teaching Castenada and a very few others that many believed he didn't exist, but one thing for certain, Castenada could not have written those teachings ascribed to Don Juan on his own. His own lifestyle betrays any idea that he gained any understanding from what he was taught.

No guide into second cognition consciousness can accurately do their jobs without resorting to what first cognitioners call polemics. A polemic is a string of verbal or written attacks against someone or something. Although Nietzsche was guilty of leveling personal polemics against certain people in some of his works, I choose to stay away from personal attacks and stay focused on the system that keeps everyone's mind enslaved. Even though I am attacking ideas and perceptions, because of how the ego takes its beliefs and embraces them as a form of its identity, many will take these writings as a personal attack, although I know no reader on a personal basis and probably never will. I am not making it personal; your own ego perception makes it personal to you.

I could write this material and name names, take pot shots at certain personalities I have alluded to, but I think making it personal tarnishes an already powerful set of messages. I have no fear of naming names; I just feel it is unnecessary cheapening of a message that stands just fine on its own. I have no desire to get into perpetual pissing matches with the gravely uninformed egos into the matters I am sharing with the public through these works. The message is too important to debase it with insults and name calling. That would serve no valid purpose. I have no personal vendetta with any of these people, only a desire to see them move past all that first cognition folly and find the door out of it. Goading someone like that while their ego is fully in place only stirs up unnecessary conflict.

If I am guilty of anything by presenting the information in these books, it is in providing years worth of my own discoveries in one explosive package to the reader. I take responsibility for maybe giving you way too much information too soon on your path, depending on how far you have progressed into your own transitional stage. On the other hand, much of this information is going to clarify so many things for those who have been doing their own research for years seeking information just like this to help them advance.

So far in this series of presentations I have not offered anything attributed to Buddha. Having explained things as in depth as I have, maybe it's time we look at a few select sayings of Buddha to see how they correspond to what I am revealing through these books.

> *"No one saves us but ourselves. No one can and no one may. We ourselves must walk the path."*

> *"There are only two mistakes one can make along the road to truth; not going at all, and not starting."*

> *"It is better to conquer yourself than to win a thousand battles. Then the victory is yours. It cannot be taken away from you, not by angels or by demons, heaven or hell."*

> *"Work out your own salvation. Do not depend on others."*

> *"It is a man's own mind, not his enemy or foe, that lures him to evil ways."*

> *"In a controversy the instant we feel anger we have already ceased striving for the truth, and have been striving for ourselves."*

> *"With fools, there is no companionship. Rather than to live with men who are selfish, vain, quarrelsome, and obstinate, let a man walk alone."*

Does there seem to be an echo occurring here? Are not these teachings the same as Jesus, Nietzsche, Don Juan and this author? I can tell you that I did not study the teachings of

Buddha in any depth over the years of my own progression and transition period. I looked into many different things, not dwelling so much on details as much as trying to find the trends of human ego belief structures - looking for a pattern to it all. To be perfectly honest, before writing the books in this series, I did not investigate very deeply into many of these teachings. It is when I was doing research for these books that I looked into and found most of the relevant teachings I am sharing with the readers at this time. I could not have given you a specific quote from Buddha or Nietzsche if my life depended on it two months ago. It is the clarity of the second cognition, coupled with internal intuitive prompts that led me to these quotes that I share with you in this series.

I know many readers will scoff at such a revelation, thinking that this is all somehow contrived, but when one is working with their spirit self - operating *as* that spirit self, and starts listening to that still silent voice within, they are led to things required in this manner. It is not dissimilar to the saying of Jesus, "Knock and it will be opened unto you."

This revelation is also relevant to one working to transition into the second cognition. Due to the insecure nature of the ego personality, we all lack a sense of self-trust in these matters. When we discover something during our progression on our path, we often find ourselves faced with an inner conflict. On one hand, a part of us recognizes on a gut level that what we discover is true, but the ego part of our first cognition thinking processes then starts sowing doubts. In most cases, we listen to that ego doubt because that is how we have lived our lives.

People will do anything to avoid the psychological discomfort of cognitive dissonance. The ego's 'voice of reason' in our heads is usually what makes us try to find that mental equilibrium that holds the ego's perceptual world together. This is why the voice of doubt originating from the ego self is so strong in all of us and so hard to overcome. What the ego uses to hold its perceptual world in place most of the time has little to do with real reason. The ego can create all sorts of unreasonable justification to convince itself that what it believes is right, meaning that it can use any sort of illogical justification to explain away the truth in favor of maintaining its own illusions. As you navigate through your own period of transition you need to be aware of this ego failing. The ego is an expert in apologetics.

When we can move past all the ego perceptions of mysticism and supernaturalism and cut to the bare bones of what enlightenment truly is, then we can finally weed out the overwrites and insertions by the first cognition misinterpreters to more clearly see the teachings for what they are and what they actually say. With this foundational understanding, we can not only see the insertions of those who misunderstood and sought to create religious or spiritual institutionalized thinking, but also how they took liberties in creating sayings that have absolutely no relevance to the second cognition whatsoever - i.e. we can see the introduction of their own personal agendas misrepresented as sayings of their teachers. When you understand the core principles of advancing consciousness, you can see the ego agendas of those who corrupted the teachings to their own selfish ends.

What has been passed down through the generations as Christianity has been illustrated through this work to have nothing whatsoever to do with the man called Jesus or what he taught. As at least one religious scholar, Hyam Maccoby has noted in his own book, *The Mythmaker: Paul and the Invention of Christianity,* what people believe to be Christianity is in actuality Paulianty, for it is the self-stated apostle Paul who spearheaded this whole thing called Christianity. I don't agree with everything Maccoby posits to support his theory in the book, but one thing is certain, Paul was a major proselytizing influence in selling the doctrine.

Saul, as he was originally called, never met Jesus. His claim to fame where Jesus is concerned is some spectacular vision he claimed to have had on the road to Damascus where purportedly, the risen Jesus told him his doctrine. Saul was supposedly so profoundly impacted by his vision that he changed his name to Paul and started creating the new institution using the name of Christ as his cover.

Paul was a Roman citizen, and his citizenship has been a point of mystery and contention by many scholars throughout the ages. The truth is not really a mystery at all. By his own writings in the New Testament, he claimed to be kin to the littlest Herod. If he was kin to the littlest Herod, then he was kin to the whole household of the Herodian kings. The religious researcher Robert Eisenman finally made the connection for Paul's Roman citizenship being due to his being a part of the House of Herod, the vassal kings of Israel put in place by the Roman Caesars. Voila! Mystery solved.

So let us take the foundation of Paul owing allegiance to Rome due to his royal family connections with the Herodian dynasty. Paul was purportedly a tent maker. Eisenman made the logical assumption that Paul made his money as a tent maker producing tents for the Roman army. If you read the Pauline doctrine of Christianity you find many Christian 'religious' teachings that were favorable to Roman rule. He wrote to pay your taxes, and for slaves to obey their masters while on earth so they could reap their heavenly rewards later, after death. Rome had suffered many slave revolts during its history, so there was a fear in the leadership of Rome that other slave revolts were always waiting in the wings to be incited. The Pauline doctrine of docility of slaves to their masters perfectly suited the Roman agenda. This is also why Nietzsche stated that Christianity was a Nihilistic religion of slavery.

I am not going to go into absolutely everything Paul did as he laid the foundations of what came to be called Christianity. If you want more understanding, just read the Pauline letters to see how he almost single-handedly shaped the character and stole the teachings of the man called Jesus and bent them totally to an agenda of mind control over the masses. Just this short illustration about the formation of the religion called Christianity compared to what Jesus taught about self-sufficiency in the second cognition are so out of tune with each other it is laughable. Make no mistake, Paul had no shortage of fellow travelers who helped put Christianity into place, but it is his letters and his words that have echoed down the halls of Christian historical doctrine to this day.

Part of what the books in this series are about is setting the historical record straight, to redeem those whose words have been misinterpreted, corrupted and abused by first cognition speculators with a personal agenda. Every reader is invited to investigate things more deeply than this series of books presents where certain areas of your interest are piqued. It is only through digging things out for yourself that you advance your own cognition. Don't simply take my word for it and try to make me into your latest authority figure. Dig into these things and prove it or disprove it for yourself. It is only through accepting this challenge that you will learn anything and hopefully turn yourself into your own authority.

Every religion on the planet has its origin in some form of mystical twaddle or another, with the possible exception of Scientology which is based on its own set of equally unrealistic beginnings and beliefs. None of them will lead you to where you are seeking to go as an independent sentiently conscious being in your own right. To follow any of these so-called religious teachings one simply makes themselves a slave to their ideologies. They all survive on the first cognition perspective of ego group-speak.

Chapter 16

*"Behold the believers of all faiths! Whom do they
hate most? The man who breaks their tablets of
values, the breaker, the lawbreaker --he, however
is the creator.
Companions, the creator seeks, not corpses--and
not herds or believers either. Fellow creators the
creator seeks -- those who write new values on
new tablets."*

Friedrich Nietzsche - Thus Spake Zarathustra

In order to advance yourself into the second cognition,
you have to be a creator. You have to be able to create yourself
anew on the rubble of the old first cognition awareness. This is
the express meaning to what Nietzsche wrote above. This being
self-created is what Jesus meant by the term being born again.
None of the teachers highlighted in these works sought followers
or believers, they sought self-created companions who might in
time stand as a beacon for all humanity to aspire to for
themselves. Only the serious spiritual seeker can tread this
pathway to self-advancement, for the process is heartbreakingly
serious and painful to all who undertake it. That is why this book
was written, to show the serious pursuer of finding their own true

self to be aware of what the process will bring you as you transition through it.

I have suffered the pain and the heartbreak of watching the world show itself for what it is during my own period of transition. I had my own beliefs shattered when they were shown to be false. I had the bouts of fear-generating cognitive dissonance, and in all honesty, sometimes it took me days to come to terms with it. As one has their perceptual illusions shattered, their mind has to make adjustments to the new information. In all honesty, these periods of adjustment vary in length, but one always comes out the other side stronger for the experience if they can recognize the falsehoods they accepted as truth all their lives.

In one sense, your transition from the first cognition into the second cognition amounts to a demolition job. To move into the second cognition could be equated with wanting to build a new house where an old one stands. You have to take a wrecking ball to the old house before you can build the new one. The transition period amounts to destroying the old house and gathering supplies to build the new one. It is not a process of having to destroy the old house before you prepare to build the new one, so navigating into the second cognition is a two-pronged approach. On one hand, you are destroying the old paradigm of illusions while you are also starting to lay the foundation for the new. You can't erode the old system without finding the information that serves as a foundation into the second cognition.

Every time you find and expose a lie that you previously believed to be truth, you are establishing the foundation for that new dwelling to house your second cognition conscious awareness. At the end of the Sermon on the Mount, Jesus used a parable to describe building this house for the second cognition as a house that's built on rock, the rock symbolizing truth. He stated that the wise builder, who does as Jesus did, builds his house on the rock, whereas the foolish man builds his house on sand and that it will be washed away. The more you research into the first cognition perceptual illusions, the more you will find that the first cognition is a house built on sand. It can't survive the scrutiny of one who truly opens their eyes to the truth and its entire foundation washes away.

As you whittle away the lies of your current perceptual beliefs, you are using the new mortar of truth to lay the foundation for your new cognitive awareness. So don't get hooked on the idea that you have to destroy first, then start to build the second house. In actuality, you will be doing both at the same time. The more you can erode that perceptual foundation of sand, the stronger the new foundation will be as you transition your consciousness away from the perceptual lies, so don't feel that as you go through this process that you are not advancing while you are destroying the old illusions. This process of advancement will most likely escape your notice at first. What I noticed on my own path to self-awareness is that I saw many things more clearly in hindsight. In the midst of my own transition, I was too close to the problem to always see the advancement I was making. I ask you to not get discouraged if you do not see immediate results, for as you tear down the old house, the tearing down is also part of your building up for the next phase of conscious development.

As I have written in this series, you have to learn to develop fluidity of thought. Even if you reach a certain state of revelation and see a new truth, don't necessarily think that it may always remain the absolute truth. Many times truths we find at one point of our transition become overshadowed when other larger truths reveal themselves to us. This doesn't necessarily mean that the lesser truth is invalid, but that you should see some truths as incomplete when you first discover them. The minor truths serve as a foundation to seeing greater truths as you progress. In many cases, they are only a smaller piece of a larger puzzle, and do not become necessarily invalid more than they become a stepping stone into a greater level of understanding.

On the other hand, you will also find things that ring true with you based on your level of cognitive advancement. In many cases, these presumed truths are exactly that - presumptions. You have to be wise enough and fluid enough to recognize when you see these errors in perception and move beyond them. Working one's way out of the ego illusion is not easy for anyone. So long as we are either operating under the ego's control, or still exercising old ego habits, we are going to fall into errors from time to time. Your spirit self is big enough to handle these mistakes. All along the way you are going to make mistakes. Accept that idea right now. No one gets through this process without a certain amount of fits and starts.. A lot of the time it feels like two steps forward and one step back.

Everyone is a creator in this process of creating themselves by becoming familiar with their inner spirit self. Everyone makes mistakes. You are going to make mistakes even as you step into the second cognition. No one is perfect in this process because until now there was nothing that remotely resembled any kind of handbook to guide people at all through this process. Even sharing my own experiences in this book will not provide you with absolutely everything you need to re-create yourself. These are merely guidelines as to what to expect that I dealt with myself and observed with others over the years. How you work all this out, what your own self-creation process turns out to be is uniquely yours. Many of you, if you have not done so already, will take some of the things that I share in this series and alter them somewhat to fit your own mold of self-creation. Others either already have, or will, create their own processes to facilitate their own growth, just as I had to create my own processes along the way. Everything about this transition is designed to show you that you are a creator, and creating yourself is the first step into becoming a creator on a greater scale.

There is no shortage of material in the New Age spiritual arena that tells people that they are creators, that they create their own reality. The problem with telling this truth to a first cognition human being is that their concept of being a creator is perceived as manifesting things in their 3D world. As I discussed in *Demystifying the Mystical,* trying to manifest and create in limited 3D reality is not going to happen as first cognition believers perceive it to be. This is why most of them fail and get frustrated when their attempts at manifesting things in the 3D reality continually fail. The first cognition concept of creating is little more than wanting to pull rabbits out of hats. It is misdirected and self-defeating, and has absolutely no value whatsoever where spiritual manifesting and creation are concerned. Operating in the first cognition, the idea that you will somehow magically make gold bars appear in your hand out of nowhere is simply a delusion. If you can't create yourself, you are not going to be able to create much of anything else, especially not something tangible like most first cognition humans expect to be able to do.

One has to get over all these mystical perceptions of magical happenings if they ever expect to advance. It is the worst form of chasing rainbows and is highly counterproductive if you want to advance your conscious awareness. In all honesty, I fell for that manifestation hype like so many others have. I did my ultimate best to manifest things in this 3D reality through sheer will power - nothing as fanciful as gold bars, but that ego part of me that still believed in the mystical hype put in a lot of effort and wasted time for no positive outcome. I want all the readers to know that if they fall for this stuff, it is because it appeals to the ego part of us that wants to be special, to show off its imagined mystical performances to others.

The ego is full of self-elevating illusions. The ego part of us can fabricate all sorts of fantastic scenarios in which or ego self is the ultimate hero. Many egos want to be like Harry Potter. They want to engage in bouts of magical duels with others. The neo-pagan belief systems, including Wicca, are rife with this crap, with people throwing spells around at each other all the time. It is all a delusional fantasy which feeds peoples egos. This is not to say that someone with high intensity ill intent can't abuse their personal energy to cause a certain amount of distress in others who may be sensitive to such energies, but for the most part, all this so-called spell casting is ritualistic practices to elevate egos. It is amazing how many people buy the trappings of magic in order to feed their ego illusions, buying everything from black candles to cast their spells to paying exorbitant prices for magic wands or the right ritual dagger, or whatever.

It goes beyond the scope of this book to get into the realistic aspects of serious energy work, and I will leave it to my wife and partner to get into that area in substantially more depth in the next volume of this series. I will only point out that there is a certain limited amount of truth in the marketplace where energy work is concerned, but it is either misdirection or simply fanciful renderings used to suck in gullible egos with a desire to perform magical acts for the sake of ego bragging rights. The path to the second cognition deals with none of this fanciful nonsense.

In this process of creating yourself, Jesus used the parable of pouring new wine into old wineskins, and how new wine poured in an old wineskin would burst. He said that one pours new wine into a new wineskin. The meaning of this parable is that you can't fit the second cognition into first cognition perception because it just doesn't fit. I used a similar analogy in this series of trying to fit 100 pounds of sugar into a 1 pound container. These are different methods of describing the same thing. You are creating a new consciousness that goes beyond the boundaries of your current awareness. This consciousness will not fit into the old first cognition container. They are incompatible and one doesn't fit inside the other.

The growing pains you are going to experience can't be avoided. There is no easy way to create yourself. A saying attributed to Buddha is probably one of the most misunderstood of his teachings based on first cognition misinterpretation. He said:

*"I have taught one thing and one thing only,
suffering and the cessation of suffering."*

The first cognition teachers of Buddha's words completely misunderstand what he was driving at in this saying. From their limited state of awareness, they always have, and still do interpret suffering in the sense of the first cognition world perception. They interpret this most important teaching as physical suffering, but what Buddha was speaking about is the suffering everyone endures from the first cognition ego manipulation. Everyone suffers at the hands of their own ego with all its doubts and anxieties, fears and discontent. The ego in

150

all of us creates more suffering around the planet than any other circumstance in which we may find ourselves. This is why he says he taught about suffering and the cessation of suffering. It is what we all suffer at the hands of the ego hijacker of our spirit's consciousness that needs cessation.

On the road to the second cognition, you are going to discover just how much suffering you have endured all your life at the hands of the ego monster inside you. Given that the ego makes one suffer even when we are unaware of it, that suffering gets amplified once you challenge the ego. The ego part of yourself is going to make you miserable every step of the way as you seek to release yourself from its stranglehold. It is often very hard to see any light at the end of the tunnel. The best I can tell you is that the light exists and it is very much worth all the suffering you will go through to gain the freedom of consciousness you are seeking.

Chapter 17

*"I tell you of three metamorphoses of the spirit:
how the spirit becomes a camel, the camel a lion,
and the lion at last a child."*

Friedrich Nietzsche - Thus Spake Zarathustra

This section of Zarathustra goes into a more poetic type rendering of the transition of these three phases of metamorphosis of spirit. If one would like to read all of Nietzsche's words in full, it is the section called *On the Three Metamorphoses* and is readily available with an online search. I am going to paraphrase what he wrote and clarify a few things that his original composition may present in a less clear fashion.

When Nietzsche refers to the spirit becoming a camel, he is referencing how your spirit self is not only strong enough to carry this burden of transition, but that it is willing to take on the burden as you transition so long as you maintain focus on your goal and remain impeccable to yourself to complete the process.

The ego part of all of us is filled with doubt and fear. Every step of the way in this process you will be met with either one or both of these tools of the ego to dissuade you from reaching your destination. Where the ego part of us is weak and willing to submit to fear and doubt, your spirit is stronger than you yet realize. Your spirit self is quite capable of carrying this heavy load, even while you have the doubts and the fears of the ego nipping at your heels at every turn. Because we don't know how strong we truly are, how strong that spirit part of ourselves truly is, we all suffer doubts, wondering whether we will ever make it, or whether there is actually any place to make it too. It is very easy to get discouraged during the transitional stage. It often feels like more burden than you can carry. Everyone goes through this without exception. We are all too heavily indoctrinated into the first cognition system to get around this hurdle. Nietzsche portrays this ego cognition as the great dragon that we must all conquer.

When we go to encounter this dragon, what Nietzsche calls 'Thou Shalt", he is talking about the entire first cognition rules of reality that have to be challenged. At this point, the lion part of your spirit says, "I will challenge this great dragon". This is the transition from the camel to the lion. This is the point in your development that after carrying the load of all that doubt and fear, those most dedicated find the strength of the lion to fight the lifelong indoctrination we have suffered at the hands of first cognition perceptual rule. We fully engage in the battle for our cognitive freedom. Everyone's spirit has that lion inside, but most are too fearful to find it. They are so indoctrinated with the rules of the first cognition - all the Thou Shalts - that they fear going against the cultural programming that is so embedded in their minds. One may find the camel for a short time, but the fear programming prohibits them from ever finding the lion in themselves.

Everyone who embarks on this journey with the pragmatism and seriousness it requires is going to come up with resistance at every turn, and this resistance is not all internal. I wrote in *Demystifying the Mystical* how many of us fall into the trap of thinking we are somehow crusaders of the truth, that we have an obligation to tell others about these things in sort of a proselytizing manner. I advised against falling into that ego trap, for that is what it is. You will save yourselves a lot of heartache if you can avoid this.

As you progress your consciousness you are going to want to share what you are learning with others, and that is where the heartache and pain begins. The vast majority of people operating in the first cognition don't want to hear anything that challenges their perceptual reality. They will think your are nuts if you try to describe what you are learning because it goes against the grain of their own first cognition indoctrination. This gets especially painful when you try to share your insights as your own consciousness advances and you can more clearly see all the folly in their actions as it unfolds to you. This is particularly hard to deal with when it is family members you are trying to share with, and how they refuse to listen. You can see how they are all trapped and enslaved by the first cognition system of awareness, and this realization creates a lot of internal angst that can serve as a hindrance if you let it override your unbending intent to succeed in the face of such adversity.

This is why the sense of detachment is so important. You have to learn to let go of trying to convince others about what you know, and you have to develop the detachment to not stay emotionally involved about whether they are going to get it or not. I am currently working with an individual that is in the transitional stage and this anxiety over how his family is treating him in regard to his own development has caused him a lot of pain. He finally realized that it is best if he just doesn't say anything to them. If you have not yet encountered this on your path, sooner or later you will, if not with family members, within your circle of friends or with your spiritual associates.

We each have to realize that the vast majority of first cognition humans are completely content to wallow in their perceived reality. It is comfortable and known to them. To advance one's spirit self on this path requires facing a lot of psychological discomfort, and in all honesty, most humans are not willing to deal with that discomfort. They don't want their perceptual world disrupted and they will do anything in their power to avoid any kind of perceptual disruption.

When we see Nietzsche refer to the Thou Shalts, most of us in the west think of Christian prohibitions because that is the Old English form of biblical prohibitions. But everywhere you turn to escape from the first cognition prison of awareness you are going to be met with Thou Shalts. They are all the rules for coloring within the cultural, political, religious and peer group liness of the first cognition. The Thou Shalts are the demands of every ego that wants a piece of you for their own selfish needs. Every ego demands nurturing of one kind or another from everyone they know. The Thou Shalts of family members are the hardest to deal with and the hardest to escape. It is because you will be met with Thou Shalts of one kind or another at every turn, both externally and internally, that you have to find that lion of your own spirit if you ever expect to succeed on your path.

This doesn't mean you have to become confrontational with everyone you know, because ultimately it is an internal battle. Learning discretion and discernment about who to talk to about these things and who to avoid broaching the subject with will often leave you with a sense of isolation. In time, you will be able to deal with this with very little problem, but while you are still combating ego habits the need for acceptance is more acute than after you pass that threshold into the second cognition. You have to remember that this quest is for total freedom of your consciousness without the necessity of others to endorse your efforts along the way. Granted, it is great if you have a partner or friend who can walk their own path beside you, but ultimately you must learn to stand alone as you create yourself anew. Loneliness is an aspect that the ego plays hard on with anyone who is trying to move their consciousness forward. The fear of having to go it alone scares most people off the path at an early stage. Other than the random loner type of personality, every ego wants some type of companionship. For the most part, the ego can't stand being by itself and the idea of that scares most egos immensely.

To not be part of the group, regardless of what kind of social circle your ego presently requires, is too much to give up for most people. Their egos can't fathom operating without the nurturing of fellow travelers in the first cognition. We are indoctrinated from our youth to be social and fit in. It is one of those Thou Shalts required in the first cognition. We are indoctrinated to not make waves, to not make a spectacle of ourselves, and the list goes on ad infinitum. Every item on this list of acceptable behavior is a Thou Shalt that the lion in you must battle and overcome. You can never become a free and independent consciousness so long as you are ruled by the first cognition diatribe of Thou Shalts that inhibit you at every turn.

Chapter 18

"Not the Height: the precipice is terrible!
The precipice, where the gaze plunges *downward*
and the hand grasps *upward.* There the heart
becomes giddy through its double will."

Friedrich Nietzsche - Thus Spake Zarathustra.

This passage expresses what I relayed earlier about how you are both destroying one house and at the same time laying the foundation for another. It is not the height of awareness that we are seeking that frightens us, but the looking downward into the first cognition that threatens to drag us back into its clutches that makes it so terrible.

First cognition awareness is like a black hole, sucking every ounce of consciousness it can into is sphere of influence. It is like a tar pit from which we are all trying to pull ourselves out. The lures of the first cognition and our lifetime of indoctrination into its reality makes looking down into it pretty frightening to anyone, but as we progress closer to the second cognition, we also get a form of giddiness the closer we get to escaping the first cognition trap.

Here is one of the major pitfalls that we all face in working to remove ourselves from that black hole of the first cognition. The ego program in all of us is extremely adaptable and malleable. Until one has fully engaged in battle with the ego, they will not discover how tricky and deceptive it can be. It can change form in the sense of ideas it will present to you to steer you off track from what you are working to achieve. As I have said before, the ego is the ultimate con man. This is why looking into the precipice is terrible. The first cognition is a house built on sand, but with the adaptable ego, those sands can shift and build a new house of the ego on a different foundation. Just as sand dunes shift in the desert, so too can the ego shift the sands of the foundation to build a new false edifice through its adaptability. I know this sounds really weird and esoteric, but I know of no other way to describe the guile of the ego perception. It is going to toss every manner of deception it can manufacture to trick you into not succeeding. The best I can advise you is to be aware of such trickery and be on guard against it when you encounter it.

One must be aware that the ego, or residual ego habits, will adapt to your advancement in an attempt to seduce you off your path. Remember what I wrote about modern gurus and how their egos deceive them after that brief encounter with an enlightenment vision. It is this exact type of deception I am talking about. It is not dissimilar to how an ego alters its game to lure people into Reiki, or how it adapts itself to accept the ritual practices of Wicca or any of the other esoteric traditions. Every one of those peoples' egos have convinced them they are on the right track, that the route they have chosen will only lead them where the ego thinks they want to go. If one decides to shift esoteric schools, the ego goes right along with it, so long as it can maintain a group identification or the sense of self-aggrandizement.

The ego is not restricted to only shifting gears in areas of mystical deception. It can just as easily resort to its own form of logic or rationale that it knows will appeal to your 'better judgment' in order to steer you off track. I realize that some readers may think I am hammering on this ego thing too much, but the fact is that what you are dealing with in your internal adversary is no joke. I can't describe every ploy it will use against you because only your ego knows how to manipulate you better than you know yourself. It is only through advancing yourself through the quagmire of ego-generated self delusions that you will finally come to understand what I am talking about. Everything else, so long as your ego is in charge, is only theoretical to you, and your ego may well convince you that it is right and I am the one who is full of it. The transition period of your development is going to be more about combating the ego and ego habits, along with the ego demands of others, than anything else, and that is why it is such a key matter for discussion while navigating your way out of the first cognition.

The precipice, as Nietzsche called it, will be a constant lure based on the fact that the first cognition is all any of us have known our whole lives. It is a vortex that continually beckons to us to come back to the herd. Every aspect of the herd mentality will be used as a negative reinforcement to lure you safely back into the fold of that known reality. The processes of criticism, ridicule, and sometimes even threats from those closest to you, are all designed by the herd to protect the herd. If you continue on your journey with fortitude, you will eventually be culled from the herd, so you may as well accept that eventuality as you progress. In essence, that is exactly what you are seeking, so get used to the idea and your transition will be a lot easier.

As you advance, you are going to find yourself being further removed from the practices of the herd. The weekend partying and socializing will eventually lose its luster when you start to see it for the shallow behavior of temporary escapism from the tedium of the first cognition herd that it is. The ego need to party it up and socialize will serve as a hindrance to one's advancement if they can't pull themselves out of that type of social black hole. Any type of social structure or gathering, if you continue to advance yourself, is going to be found more tedious than you may yet understand. As your consciousness advances you will see the egos all on display and what games each ego plays to get its attention. In time, you will find these ego displays utterly tiresome because they are all just to emotionally taxing.

Egos feed off other egos. You are going to discover how needy every ego is in one capacity or another. It is easy to see the really needy egos, the clinging, smothering types. But in time, you will recognize that every ego is just as needy and demanding in its own cries for attention. You are eventually going to get sick of dealing with the nonsense, and this is the point you start turning yourself into somewhat of a hermit just to escape the constant grabbing at your emotions to feed all their illusions.

Every ego is an emotional manipulator, whether they manipulate through wheedling and whining, or they manipulate through displays of angry outbursts or through exhibiting other behaviors that generate sympathy for them. Egos manipulate and corrupt every emotion. The more you see this manipulation, the more you are going to want to avoid it, but until you do, that lure is always there to drag you back down into the pit of the first cognition. Again, this is why emotional detachment is so very important. So long as you can be emotionally manipulated by others, through guilt, anger, fear and even the ego perception of love, you are walking a tightrope. This is why the ones closest to you, in many regards, present the greatest impediment to your advancement. They are the anchor that our own egos are most reluctant to cut those emotionally manipulative ties with.

By saying these things, I'm not advising anyone to desert their families, get divorced or any such thing. If you have a good relationship, you should be able to do your work without destroying a marriage relationship. Much of that is going to rely on your partner and how they can deal with the changes in you. Truthfully, in some cases relationships do dissolve, but I do not advocate that one should approach their personal advancement with an eye toward necessary destruction of such relationships.

Sometimes it happens, sometimes it doesn't, so don't dread personal advancement thinking it is any kind of requirement.

To gain emotional detachment doesn't mean you stop loving people, it just means you are advancing into a greater understanding of emotions without the ego manipulating them as a form of reaction. What the ego perceives love to be is a need. The ego needs love to validate itself as being lovable, but the ego also uses love to control others. The ego desire for love, as it perceives it, is like a drug. The ego form of love eventually pales, and this is why the ego loves to fall in love. It is the emotional intensity of falling in love that generates the strongest emotion for the ego to feed on. Love is also a powerful enough emotion to feed the inorganic beings. That is why the whole New Age arena is saturated with sickeningly sweet love and light and the group hugs and everything else. It is emotional nourishment to the subset of the herd egos and also energetic nourishment to certain elements of the inorganics.

Love sells. Who can argue with love? What is bad about love? Why should I even throw love into this discussion? Don't I know how to love? These are all questions posed by egos hooked on the first cognition *perception* of love. If everything in the first cognition is in fact perception, as I assert, then love is not exempt from that perceptual framework. Real love, love as it is understood by your spirit self, is not needy, clingy or manipulative. Until you can get your emotions in balance, which occurs as a natural part of your process of advancement, you can't understand love or any other emotion as anything more than a *perceptual illusion.*

All you understand about love, hate, anger or guilt is what the ego manipulates you into believing these emotions are. The ego has no understanding of spirit, so all it can do is produce counterfeits of everything - and that includes all your emotions. Emotions as you currently understand them, operating within the first cognition, are only cheap imitations of the real thing. Under the influence of the ego, the whole world is blinded by emotions. This doesn't mean that one is just in a state of heightened emotional reactivity as it is normally interpreted. In truth it means that people are blinded by the perceptual illusion generated by the ego imitating real emotions. How you perceive your emotions is as unreal as every other perception in the first cognition. Until you advance to the point you can see and understand this, your emotions are the anchor that can drag you back into the first cognition during any phase of the transition period of your development. Your spirit is not a sucker for love, but your ego definitely is.

Chapter 19

"Whether they be servile before gods and divine kicks, or before men and the stupid opinions of men: it spits at *all* kinds of slaves, this blessed selfishness!"

Friedrich Nietzsche - Thus Spake Zarathustra

Throughout this series of books I have emphasized how we all start out as slaves to the first cognition. I also wrote in *Demystifying the Mystical* how one needs to become self-centered in a spiritual sense, to be selfish in regard to connecting with the spirit that lies within all of us. I do not disrespect any person for who they are, but I do disrespect the wanton ignorance their egos project on the world. I detest and spit at the toxic emotions they dump into the collective environment every hour of every day just so their egos can feel justified in its existence.

The egos scream and stamp their feet and beat their breasts to be seen and deemed the best at whatever the ego wants to be best at. They launch emotional assaults in words through voice as well as through the written word. They are all defenders of the petty fiefdom of their own blustering egos and the fragile perceptual world that nurtures them. Even if you have not yet crossed over into the second cognition, given all that I have explained in this series, how can we continue to give credence to a world governed by such arrogance and idiocy? If you are seeking your own conscious advancement without all the egos pulling and pushing at you through every emotional manipulation imaginable, then how can you ever hope to succeed if you don't selfishly safeguard the domain of your spirit self?

You can't share this with the herd, for they will burn you down any way they can. They will rip you apart through emotional manipulation in order to keep you in the herd, playing the same shallow mind games they play with themselves day in and day out. Everyone plays their own type of ego mind games. We are trained how to do that as a form of social survival. I did it too. If you are honest, so do you in one degree or another. The question you have to ask yourself is whether you are going to be content living your entire life this way until you get the dirt blanket at the end of the line, or whether you seek something more wholesome and realistic in the alternative?

The perceptual world of the ego is like a mass psychosis with the inmates running the asylum. The defenders of the faith, the protectors of the realm of consciousness of the first cognition, will do everything they can to fix you and make you a workable cog in their perceptual machine. The philosophy-based psychologists and psychiatrists know all the definitions about what is normal and acceptable in that perceptual realm. They are the hard-line realists that *really* know what reality is about, right?

They are the speculative gatekeepers for the first cognition. If the rest of the herd can't force you into the compliance of normalcy, by God the shrinks sure can! They are the experts! If they don't have a definition for your particular ego perceptual delusion, one of them will surely frame a new diagnosis to classify it.

Through their no nonsense approach to reality, none of the things I am relating in this series can be remotely real in their world of speculation and definitions of reality. Have no doubt that some would love to put me on their couch to dissect my mind and find out some way to classify my state of 'delusion' according to their standards of reality. There are already too many of us who are looking for that doorway out of their limited perceptual reality to make ourselves lab rats to their limited cognition. Most do not understand what it is that is driving this push to spiritual understanding within themselves, and the watchmen of the first cognition stand guard to insure no one escapes their rigidly defined cognitive reality. The guards are not going to provide any answer that doesn't put one safely back as a cog in their cognitive machine.

If you have been on this path of self-discovery for any length of time you have already been confronted at every turn with their stalwart denials, their abusive criticisms and the personal insults because that is how they protect their reality of Thou Shalts. Throughout human history they have burned presumed witches and crucified all the wave-makers in their reality. They can more readily suffer tyrants than they can anyone they *think* is remotely better than their own ego perceptions of themselves.

Psychologists and psychiatrists define what is acceptable in that reality. To them, there is no such thing as higher cognitive awareness if they can't fit it into the pre-defined parameters of their books and rules of psychology, which are all written by the same kind of limited cognition 'authorities'. It is a closed loop disaster for human consciousness. The scientists of the first cognition are no better, desiring to hook up measuring devices and probes to hopefully understand the brain as the seat of consciousness. They can't comprehend states of higher consciousness even when they hook their machines up to habitual meditators whose altered brain waves show their machines 'something', but the scientists do not have the cognitive capability to remotely understand what any of this means without trying to fit it all into the acceptable framework of first cognition reality.

Everyone operating from their own ego is a staunch defender of their own brand of the first cognition reality, no matter how illogical that perception may be, which includes the fascination with the mystical, magical and supernatural. They live in a constant search for external authority, ultimately seeking the greatest authority found in their perceptions of one god or another, or a belief in the sacred or divine. All of these varied frameworks of perception in the first cognition are purely rational to the individual ego mind, and even the practices of reason and logic as they are applied in the scientific and pseudoscientific mind sciences utterly fail them when it comes to remotely comprehending the possibility of a higher level cognitive awareness that exists outside their limited perceptual boxes.

The egos of the first cognition can't tolerate the idea that they can be remotely wrong. The more powerfully one can provide them the evidence of the errors of the whole paradigm, the more their hackles rise to protect the system and destroy the messenger through any means possible. As you work to circumvent this system to achieve your own cognitive advancement, the slings and arrows of their dissent will confront you at every turn if you try to be remotely truthful with them. It is best that you learn to keep your own counsel and spare yourself the misery of castings pearls before swine.

I am re-engaging these points because it is the price exacted from all first cognition protectors of their perceptual faith against anyone who tries to leave the herd. Sadly, too many cave into the pressure and cease their journeys altogether. Only those with the keenest will to power, whose spirits can claim the strength of the lion to fight this fight to its proper ending will succeed. This is why I have reiterated throughout this series that you are going to have to be very courageous if you intend to succeed in your efforts. It is due to this constant resistance by and negative reinforcement from the defenders of the first cognition that the weak are ultimately weeded out and fall back into a sort of dissatisfied existence in their world.

Every one of the staunch defenders of the first cognition are unwitting slaves in their ego-imprisoned awareness. Their opinions, their faiths, their beliefs in their gods and every ounce of supernatural folderol are utterly meaningless in a grander perceptual view. The consciousness of the ego is a spoiled brat, regardless of whether it inhabits an adult body and no matter how much accumulated knowledge it may claim to posses. Each and every one of them may have knowledge of many things within that limited perceptual world, but they have no real comprehension of anything beyond that without resorting to defining it as metaphysical or mystical.

If *any* human being can experience any of the things I have written about, then the possibility is there for *all* human beings to do so. This makes it patently pragmatic and most definitely not supernatural. It is only a natural process for anyone who seeks to attain it by doing the necessary work to remove all the ego cognitive illusions that hold us all enslaved. What makes it seem unnatural is the unnatural perception of the ego. It is the ego counterfeiter that we have allowed to define a counterfeit perception of reality designed to cater to its own self-indulgent ends. It is because of this inherent egoistic self-centered selfishness that inorganic consciousnesses can so easily play an ego consciousness like a fiddle. The inorganics play to the weaknesses and counterfeit desires of the most base of human emotions - greed in all its forms, the need to be special, the need to feel powerful in the realm of other egos, and most of all, that smug sense of self-gratification and validation that every ego requires to survive. The term 'feeding the ego' has the keenest relevance when viewed in this manner. Everyone's ego seeks to be fed one form of validating malarkey or another. It is what keeps it firmly seated on the throne in everyone's head - until they oust the tyrant and claim their birthright as a truly free spiritual being.

Chapter 20

"The great disgust with man -- *it* choked me and
had crept into my throat: and what the soothsayer
truly said: "All is the same, nothing is worthwhile,
knowledge chokes."

Friedrich Nietzsche - Thus Spake Zarathustra

On your path to spiritual self-awareness you are going to reach a place of disgust with the world that surrounds you. As you work to remove the control of your own ego, you are going to be more acutely aware of the ego in everyone else. You are going to be assaulted with all the 'knowledge' of the army of egos who protect the perceptual world of the first cognition. It is very easy when one reaches this stage of their development to become very disenchanted with the whole process of spiritual advancement. You will wonder what's the use in progressing onward if you are still going to be surrounded and bound in such a world of fruitless folly.

This is a most difficult stage of navigating into the second cognition because you have technically reached the point of no return. When you find yourself at this stage of your development, you already know too much about the system to gracefully fall back into it. When you reach this stage, you are truly in that no man's land between the first and second cognitions. You know you can't go back, no matter how hard you might try, and moving forward feels hopeless because you can't yet see any light at the end of the tunnel. It is usually during this phase of personal disenchantment that people try to just plain quit on spirit work. I quit more than once during this hard part of my own transition. This is much like the challenge that Trinity leveled at Neo when he tried to get out of the car and walk away and she said something to the effect, "You have been down that road before, is that really what you want?"

When you reach this no man's land, and you look back into the world of the first cognition, you finally realize you have reached that threshold where forward is the only way to move. You may quit, as I did, but it won't last long for the simple reason that there is nothing to go back to in the world of the first cognition. You already see it and recognize it for what it is, and there is absolutely no way in good conscience that you can ever re-embrace that world. This mirrors the question that Morpheus asked Neo when Neo realized that he couldn't go back, "Even if you could go back, would you want to?"

This period of the transition always brings one a sense of internal conflict. It is not cognitive dissonance, but a conflict in decisions. When you start the spirit path you are making superficial decisions to follow whatever path you choose based on ego desires. Such decisions are based mostly on fanciful notions more than they arise from any sense of deep commitment. The ego can change beliefs as easily as one can change clothing if it suits the ego's agenda. It can move from Christianity to Wicca or other New Age forms of spiritual thinking without a lot of cognitive hassle. There is no real internal conflict from these decisions, at least not much more conflict than trying to decide what model of car you want to buy.

There is a point on every serious seeker's path that they have to make an informed decision. They have to make a commitment to the spirit self inside that they are going to go the distance no matter how much crap is tossed in your way to dissuade you. If you have not made such a commitment before you hit this no man's land in your transition, you are most likely going to have to make that commitment to spiritual advancement in order to proceed.

When I met my wife, she happened to be at that decision point. She was all ramped up and angry because spirit hadn't delivered what she 'expected' and she was off on a real tear over this. Most people who are truly seeking to advance themselves reach this point sooner or later in their development. They have come up with preconceived notions about what spirituality is and they build expectations about what they are supposed to get in return for all their efforts. None of these expectations are remotely true, but we all fabricate them in our minds and our egos play with all sorts of fanciful notions to keep us engaged in these false expectations.

My wife and I went round and round for over 4 hours, and I kept reiterating to her that she was at that point in her spiritual development that she was going to have to make that decision of commitment if she expected to get unstuck. Her disenchantment with the process, her anger that 'spirit' hadn't delivered on the promises her ego had fabricated in her mind, kept her recriminating and blaming spirit for the expectations her ego had built in her imagination. Although her ego was venting against 'spirit', it had nothing to do with spirit and everything to do with shattered ego expectations. I share this story with you to illustrate how the ego first builds its house of illusions by creating false expectations, and how it blames anyone it can when its own fabricated expectations fail to manifest the way ego wants it to be. My wife finally made that commitment to her spiritual growth, and her path has been ever-expanding ever since.

This goes back to the chapter header for this section. We all get our heads full of presumed knowledge, particularly in matters of spirit, yet all this presumed knowledge is actually no real knowledge at all. Everyone builds expectations. How many times in your life have you said or heard others says, "I didn't expect that." Building expectations is one of the primary habits of the ego and it is one that is very hard to break. Expectations of all kinds generally lead to disappointment. In matters of spirit, expectations erected by the ego imagination *always* fail. This is why I instruct people to avoid expectations in matters of spirit in order to avoid such disappointments. It was the shattered expectations created by accepting presumed knowledge of the speculators in the realm of spirit that misguided me and misguides everyone on the spirit path. Every single aspect of spiritual *knowledge* in the first cognition, whether it be religious or mystical, is a set up for disappointment because every one of them is built on false expectations.

One of the last and hardest bouts of cognitive dissonance that occurred within myself was when I finally realized once and for all that all the spiritual traditions presented in the first cognition were utter and complete bullshit. This realization after about 16-18 years on my own path really rocked my perceptual world. I got angry because I and bought into and dedicated myself to the malarkey for so long. The sense of self-betrayal and utter gullibility I felt in believing it all for so long was the last and hardest pill I had to swallow where it came to undoing my own personal perceptual boundaries of the first cognition.

Unlike most people playing around with spiritual teachings, I was always serious from the start. I was never a spiritual tourist or weekend warrior once I started my own quest. I had the internal drive and determination to stay focused on it every step of the way. What I am trying to describe in this volume of the series is how you will come to certain realizations and how you are liable to react to many of them. In most cases we feel we are utterly alone in this process, unless you are as fortunate as I was to have a partner progressing on her own path beside me. Many people progress this path quite alone and still succeed in pushing through.

What drives one, what keeps one moving forward, in my estimation, is information. On my own path I sought information through many avenues seeking understanding. In hindsight I can see how much of what I came to understand was a result of intuitively reading between the lines of the information I hungrily sought after. In many respects, walking the spirit path to the second cognition amounts to being a form of detective work, gleaning over volumes of material seeking clues that can clear the world of misperceptions. The more astute one becomes at reading between the lines from an intuitive standpoint, the more one will advance learning to glean such clues, if they are present in what you are researching. It is like a game of connect the dots, with most of the dots being intentionally erased where the information we need has been tampered with. This is another reason that advancing one's conscious awareness is so damnably hard.

We have been indoctrinated since childhood to accept the voices of our authority figures. We develop a misplaced trust that our authorities are telling us the truth, when in most cases they are as vastly ill informed as we are individually. This goes back to that blind leading the blind parable posed by Jesus. We all get indoctrinated at an early age to simply accept the words of our authorities simply because they are authorities. It is only when one starts to develop critical thinking skills that they start to look beyond the facial presentations of facts to seeking answers more deeply. We take things at face value all too often. To advance into the second cognition, you realize that nothing is as it appears. It is all perceptual fallacy.

Wherever we turn we are bombarded with statements of *knowledge* by our authority figures, yet throughout the history of mankind, none of these men and women of knowledge have advanced their consciousness one iota. This is what Nietzsche means about being choked by knowledge. Just look at the people you know, how many of you can dictate useless knowledge about songs, bands, actors and actresses, who they are married to, what the latest scandal is, what politicians do or don't do, etc., etc.? Our heads are filled with meaningless facts and we all act like this knowledge is important. I have repeatedly expressed the knowledge of how to do something from experience is exponentially more valuable knowledge than all the memorizing and book learning of remembering hollow 'facts'. Such knowledge, or professing such knowledge is as meaningless as keeping up with the Hollywood stars.

Our academics and teachers can spout out quotes and authoritative references of who said what, and this personal inventory of facts or figures is what makes them an authority on *knowledge.* So you can recite poems of Emily Dickenson or Ralph Waldo Emerson, what the hell good does it do your cognitive advancement? It is simply an exercise in memorizing something that appeals to your ego. Reciting the information gratifies the ego as being more knowledgeable than the person who can't pull quotes out of their behind to challenge you. This is the measure of *knowledge* in the first cognition, and none of this type of knowledge is founded in any experience beyond simple memorization. It is all superficial posturing for one ego to come off more superior to another.

Everyone is an expert on what they know about what they think and believe. I get so tired of people in the spiritual arena claiming they know this about spirit and that about spirit, when in actuality, they are only parroting the words of others who don't *know* any more than those parroting them profess to know. It is this mistaken sense of knowledge at all levels that keeps humanity handicapped and groveling at the feet of the first cognition, protecting the world that has enslaved their minds. This form of knowledge is as counterfeit as every other perception created and enforced by ego personalities everywhere. How can one not feel choked and disgusted in the face of this realization? The world of our presumed knowledge is smothering all of us in useless and needless facts and figures, and we all play the game thinking this somehow makes us appear to be knowledgeable.

All of this is the world you will look back on when you reach the no man's land. If you have not done so by that point, you will need to make that ultimate commitment to your spirit self to move forward, or you may well wind up stuck and miserable in that place. This is what I call the 'choice point' that everyone on the spirit path must ultimately decide. You have to remember, this commitment is to your own cognitive advancement. You are not committing to anything or anyone but your spirit self, but without that irrevocable and total commitment, you are only going to progress so far. With spirit, you are either all in or all out once you reach that decision point. There are no halfway measures, no partial commitments to your spirit self. You either do it or you don't.

People confront this choice point at different stages of their development. This point of commitment comes sooner for some and later for others, but everyone must ultimately make that choice if they expect to advance. You are in a war between two separate forms of consciousness, on one hand you have the ego, and on the other hand you have your spirit. One can't serve two masters, meaning that you can't serve the ego and find your spiritual freedom at the same time, so each of us has to make that final decision as to which part of ourselves we are going to commit to, our ego or our spirit self. So long as you remain indecisive and unwilling to commit, your spirit self is not obligated to pressure you into jumping one way or the other. The choice must be made from the standpoint of a conscious decision of each individual in an incarnation.

Your spirit self is who it is. It knows who it is, but the consciousness that controls us during an incarnation is the experience-driver to enhance each individual spirit. If you want to realize your spirit self while in human form, you have to make the conscious and deliberate choice to do so as a statement of intent that this is an experience you desire during *this* incarnation. The consciousness of your spirit won't force this decision on you. It remains available if you commit yourself to experiencing it, but not unless you fully commit to the decision.

Do not construe this as any type of compelled performance, because there is nothing compelling you to make this choice except your own conscious decision-making capability. You are exercising a free will choice to either do this or not do it. It is no different than any other major life decision that requires a commitment, such as marriage, for example. Once you commit to the decision, abide by it and your spirit self will honor that contract with yourself. Don't make the commitment if you have any doubts about the process and your willingness to fulfill your agreement to do so. You can't lie to yourself in this matter. It is like Yoda said to Luke Skywalker, "Either do or do not do, there is no try."

Chapter 21

"But only man is hard to bear! That is because he carries too much that is foreign on his shoulders. Like the camel he kneels down and lets himself be well laden.
Especially the strong, reverent spirit who would bear much: he loads too many *foreign* weighty words and values upon himself--now life seems like a desert to him!"

Friedrich Nietzsche - Thus Spake Zarathustra

We hear much about human nature. We accept certain principles about presumed human nature by our many and varied experts into the human psyche. I am here to tell you that we perceive nothing about true human nature, all we project as the knowledge of human nature is nothing but an expression of *ego nature*. We humans have never discovered true human nature because we have been enslaved by the first cognition perceptions of the ego since mankind appeared on this planet at the beginning.

We are all so controlled and weighted down with the foreign concepts of ego nature that very few of us have ever transcended into the second cognition to truly comprehend what human nature is, absent the vile and possessing ego. Everywhere we look, every corner we turn anywhere on this planet, we are not met with human nature, we are met by people enslaved by ego nature. It is also those entrapped and ensnared in the same system of ego perceptions that tell us what they presume human nature to be. Have I not stated repeatedly throughout this series that the ego is hopelessly predictable? It is exactly because of this predictable nature of the ego perception that anything as lame as a definition of human nature to describe the predictable nature of the ego can even find merit.

Like everything else, presumed human nature is a counterfeit projection of a false personality demanding adherence to its systems of false perceptual values. We do not know what true human nature is because so few have transcended their cognitive awareness to understand what a *real* human being is with a fully functional and free consciousness. We are left with insufficient interpretations of what human nature is predicated on the interpretations of human egos locked into this dreadful prison of ego consciousness. One does not have to even get close to the second cognition to perceive the first cognition as a barren desert.

Human nature, as it is currently labeled and understood, is controlled by a counterfeit perception of a greater reality, which a fully developed human in the second cognition can see clearly. What we describe as human nature is a sham, it is but a caricature of what can be, but has not yet been realized where humanity as a whole is concerned. Human nature as it is currently perceived is a dancing robot, a pale replica of what humans can truly be if they can defeat the ego hacker consciousness that rules our minds and our current perceptions.

Don Juan taught that we are "all simply making figures in front of a mirror." The meaning of this observation about humanity in general is the fact that we are all putting on a front, an act predicated on appearances to everyone we meet, whose eyes are simply reflections for our own egos. We are all putting on a specific personal performance, making useless gestures in front of a mirror of the eyes of others. This is not human nature, this is the nature and reason for existence for every ego on the planet. It is the superficial presentation of appearances between egos. How they act, what they do, the lengths they go to seeking external approval are all just fruitless gestures designed to bolster and reinforce their own ego image of themselves. Everyone is an actor and, as the saying goes, the whole world is the stage for these hollow actions of egos. In light of acknowledging these facts, how can it remotely be described as human nature? It is all the nature of a foreign invading consciousness that has no real basis on its own. It is a program, and every mind on the planet has been hacked by this program. It is a mind virus, a collective consciousness meme.

We have all been burdened to the point of breaking with all the rules and regulations of our consciousness through the dictates of this hacker program. This world does not now, nor ever has belonged to real human beings. It is the perceptual domain of the ego program. It is a world filled with greed and avarice, murder, theft and warfare. It is a world of competition between egos all striving for their own piece of the perceptual pie. We don't know our true nature, our human nature, because we are not humans, we are egos pretending to be human.

Under the burden of the ego system, each and every one of us is prevented from becoming acquainted with our humanity. We live in an inhumane world for that is the world of the ego. It is inhumane because the ego is *not* human. The ego is an unnatural overlay on our human consciousness, and we start the indoctrination process into its world within days after we are born. Before we can even speak we start observing the habits of ego indoctrination by watching the ego interchanges of our parents and others we are carried around to and shared with as babies. When we start to talk, the ego indoctrination to the operating rules in its world really start to be hammered into us. In truth, we probably only have a matter of a few days after we are born that we are ever really human. After that, the indoctrination starts and we are turned into ego slaves, defenders of the system, hopelessly brainwashed and horribly never being aware of the fact that we are brainwashed. This is why one who has found their humanity finds man so hard to bear.

As you are navigating your way into the second cognition these realizations are going to become more poignant. Your sense of the wrongness of it all will become amplified to the point that moving forward seems utterly pointless. During the transition period, we have a hard time perceiving how we will be able to function in that world anymore given what we have learned about the fruitlessness of it all. A sort of despair sets in and we feel we can't go on. We see the utter senselessness of the whole system and we feel that we can no longer function within that system. This is a very hard part of the transition because you can't just throw in the towel and quit living. You can't just up and quit your job and go find a cabin or a cave to live in to escape the insanity, and you will find yourself forcing yourself to go in and face your job every day. You are going to have to find the courage of the lion to continue your normal routines as you pass over this abyss of realization. In time, the despair you feel will pass as you gain that spiritual balance and cognitive equilibrium, but I am not going to lie to you, this is a very tough transitional point that everyone I know eventually encountered.

Regardless of your transition into the second cognition, you are still going to have to function in this world of madness just to pay your bills and put food on the table. As hard as it is to force yourself to maintain your necessary routines for survival, you are just plain going to have to have the strength to get through this adjustment in your transition. You are going to have to become adept at what Don Juan called controlled folly, which means that even though you know the perceptual world around you means nothing and is all folly of the ego perception, you are going to have to put on the brave front to survive in it. We all have to do what is necessary to survive. The difference is that operating under the control of our ego we don't know the difference. It is still a world of perceptual folly, but while the ego controls us, we don't see the desert for what it is.

Once you finally cross over into the second cognition these situations will be easier to deal with, but until you get there, it is going to cause you a lot of mental discomfort. By the time you have transitioned fully into the second cognition you will have developed the necessary detachment to be able to deal with the ego idiocy better, and you will also learn to not put yourself in situations where you don't have to deal with it. What I mentioned previously about partying and social gatherings is relevant in understanding this. Although at this point of your development, you may be highly concerned about not wanting or having that kind of ego-nurturing interfacing, one comes to accept it with an equanimity I can't fully describe where you will understand it. Just know that as uncomfortable as it may sound to you at the moment, depending on your own current level of development, this dependency of interaction with others will fade and you will do quite well on your own, and you won't really miss it after the fact.

It would be a much better world if our authorities and dictators of reality could come to the party of higher level cognitive awareness, then maybe we could start to see a redefining of human nature versus ego nature. I have defined the difference in this book. The only question that remains is how many psychologists and psychiatrists who make these definitions will hear the call and turn themselves into real human beings rather than remaining ego-controlled human counterfeits.

Chapter 22

"Disguised I sat among them, ready to
misunderstand *myself* that I might endure *them,*
and gladly saying to myself: "You fool, you do
not know men!"
One forgets about men when one lives among
them: there is too much foreground in all men --
what can far-seeing, far-seeking eyes do *there*!"

Friedrich Nietzsche - Thus Spake Zarathustra

Living in the world of the first cognition we are all in disguise. We are all hiding behind the mask of our own egos. Just as Nietzsche said, we are all willing to misunderstand ourselves in order to try and understand them - strictly from the perspectives of our egos. The ego in all of us forces to comply with the rules of our perceptual realities, and we are all trying to fit into and abide by the rules of ego survival. In the world of the ego, survival of the fittest is the mentality that rules, but being the fittest in that world does not mean the most healthy. The fittest in the world of the ego are the abusers, the rapists, the thieves, the murderers, not just of other men, but the murderers of any new idea or concept that pokes at that ego reality.

Everyone is vain to a certain degree in the ego world paradigm. Only the most vain get labeled as such, but every ego is self-glorifying and seeking attention, and in that regard, we are all vain. We may each deny this observation, but in the light of total personal honesty, none of us can really deny it. If you are dressing for any type of image projection, it is a form of personal vanity, if for no other reason than to be acceptable in the eyes of others. The fear of criticism or non-acceptance by the herd makes everyone vain to a certain degree. Our cultures set the rules of acceptable behavior and attire, from the most primitive tribes in the jungles around the world to the larger tribes of nations, the ego program sets all the rules we must live by.

Within this over-regulated and overburdened perceptual world, how far is anyone truly allowed to *see* without running up against the herd enforcers? When one develops the cognitive awareness to see farther and seek more, what is there in the perceptual world of the first cognition that is worth holding our cognitive attention? Does the ego world really feed our spirits, our souls, or does it merely feed itself with its own perceptual illusions and rules? If you have read all the volumes in this series, the answer is patently obvious.

Under the first cognition, we all live in a barren wasteland for our consciousness. No matter which direction we turn, we are met with its cultural rules and boundaries. We are told to think outside the box, but the harsh truth is, we are not expected to think so far outside that perceptual box that we threaten the entire perceptual reality. Moving into the second cognition is not thinking outside the box, it is destroying the perceptual box of the ego world in its entirety where your own cognitive awareness is concerned. You can't make other people get it, so don't even try. Leave their minds to wallow in the wasteland of their own limited perceptions and move ahead without them. If you wait on them, if you think you can't move forward out of some misguided belief that staying behind to help humanity get it holds some noble purpose, it is only your ego deluding you with self-pride and your own sense of self-importance. There is no value in being the last man standing in the first cognition. I would rather be the first one through the gate than stay behind to prod the others.

As I write these books, I am not standing still in my own progression. I continue to advance with or without others, and I am not looking back. If you can't find that same kind of focus within yourself, then it is going to take you longer in this process, provided you work to complete it at all. These books are all being written primarily for those who have already discovered a lot of these things for themselves. They are not written for the novices, the spiritual tourists, nor the harsh defenders of the first cognition. I have no desire to save the world, nor am I on a personal crusade to convert anyone to anything more than knowing themselves.

These books are written primarily for those already deep into their personal quest to provide information in a marketplace where such information is totally lacking. I am sharing the parables and sayings of the ancient teachers in an attempt to vindicate their teachings, to show the dogmatists and the mystical-minded of this generation just how we have been buffaloed by our limited system of cognition. I am placing the teachings of Jesus, Buddha, Nietzsche and Don Juan were they need to be, squarely front and center as beacons to the second cognition. I am taking their teachings and presenting them for what they actually mean rather than the lame dogmatizing and speculating done by lesser minds operating in the first cognition, most of whom had their own agendas of control when they misinterpreted the true meaning of the teachings.

It is true that their messages were not as concise and clear as they are explained in these volumes, yet we have a dual failing in understanding the meaning of their teachings. On one hand, they were open to misinterpretation. On the other hand, we take how we think today and try to project the same process into historical arenas for which we have no real understanding. Jesus and Buddha spoke in parables and stories because that is what an illiterate populace understood best at those times and within those cultures. So little survives from a historical standpoint of those ancient days that we have very little understanding of how their world was in comparison to ours. So our historians and authorities project their modern suppositions onto the ancient societies and we presume they are correct. Both of these noted failings are why to this day, where the 'mystical' teachings are concerned, no one can understand them.

Take the foregoing failings, then remember what I wrote about the first cognition having no point of relationship with the second cognition to even frame a comparative analogy, and we arrive at why no one knows squat about the second cognition. I have no doubt that there are some on this planet who have already crossed into the second cognition, but none of them are the presumed authorities who write books or do speaking engagements, either academics or spiritual teachers. As I clearly stated in *Willful Evolution*, *"there are no current qualified authorities* on the subject of expanded cognitive awareness."

The theorists and the speculators, once they get their hands on this material, and make no mistake, some will, will only be able to issue challenges and disparaging attacks and denials, yet not a one of them can refute the information in these books. None of them possess the foundational knowledge to even comprehend the second cognition, let alone be qualified to challenge the information without simply trying to destroy the message. If they had knowledge of the second cognition, they couldn't refute it - they wouldn't want to. So that leaves the first cognition naysayers to poke holes at something they have zero authority to challenge.

The authorities of the first cognition can't refute the reality of the second cognition with their math or physics, they can't refute it by citing their favored philosophers or psychologists, and they have no other information at their disposal that can prove it wrong in any manner, but have no doubt, they will try to destroy the messages in these books, just as first cognitioners have throughout the ages.

Having said these things, it is not about me. None of this work is about me, it is about those who are going to succeed. The foregoing statements, if anything, are an indictment against all authorities of the first cognition who can only destroy what they cannot or will not try to understand. If the predicted actions come forth against these writings, they only validate everything I am writing against the entire system of the first cognition. Jesus' saying, "By their deeds shall ye know them," will have resounding effect to the readers of these volumes to transition themselves despite the authoritative voices who will try to silence or discredit the work.

I made these forecasts about their actions because they are simply predictable actions of the ego defenders based on their repetitive reactions over the ages. Their own egos will not allow them to stand silent in the face of such observations. I am not paranoid in saying these things. I do not fear their words of authority nor the awards and diplomas they wave as their claim for that authority. I am simply making a projection based on the predictable nature of authoritarian egos throughout time. In all honesty, I would be more surprised if they didn't challenge the work.

The ego in all of us hates criticism. It particularly hates being proven wrong and becomes embarrassed or mortified. Embarrassment is a form of shame programming that is deeply embedded in every human around the world. One may try to argue with this observation, but how many times in your life have you heard, "You ought to be ashamed of yourself!", or

"Have you no shame?" No ego wants to 'get caught' doing certain things because of the known shame reaction that comes with its actions being discovered. Shame is one of the most pernicious programs ever designed for cultural, and especially religious enforcement of all the Thou Shalts of the first cognition. Shame in and of itself is its own form of punishment, creating a mental angst in virtually all humans when it is used against us by the protectors of the herd mentality.

As all the readers must know, now that I have pointed out the power of shame programming, we were all introduced to this particular form of Thou Shalt at our earliest ages. The shame programming is plugged in so early in our lives that it is one of the primary and major programs that everyone carries all their lives. Many of the other overlaid programs of the ego world can be just as pernicious, but shame programming is the oldest and most deeply embedded reactive program of first cognition societies everywhere. It is a form of shame programming that creates the sense of embarrassment that every ego experiences when proven to be wrong or made to feel foolish. It is a shame reaction from being caught at whatever led to that discovery by someone else - being made to feel foolish at discovering that you walked all the way to work with your skirt tucked into the back of your pantyhose, as just one example. Each reader can fill in the blanks of any certain experience of shame programming in their own lives and see how the enforcement programming works.

It is a tangential form of shame programming that bullies everywhere use to destroy the self esteem of fragile egos. It is a form of shame programming when authority figures ridicule others because of their lack of education compared to the degrees hanging on their own walls. Shame programming is a very important control mechanism for maintaining the first cognition perception of reality. When any ego attacks another ego, at the base of the desired reaction you will find shame. For all of our lives through untold numbers of experiences, we are all shamed into compliance with the system. As stated, embarrassment is a form of shame programming, and no ego wants to feel shamed through embarrassment. Because every ego knows what it feels like to be shamed, every ego also knows exactly how to project shame on others to win their arguments. They may not recognize it as shaming, but when you take it to its base element, but forcing someone into an admission that agrees with yours amounts to shaming them into compliance. Whenever one seeks to make another feel small, shame is the weapon of choice in the first cognition.

I bring up shame programming at this point to instruct the reader that when they encounter opposition to what they are trying to achieve at the hands of first cognition detractors, that shame in one form or another will be used as a pressure tactic to keep you firmly rooted in the herd mentality. They may not actually use the word shame in their accusations, but shame programming takes on many faces. Shame programming is used to make one feel uncertain, to question themselves in the face of opposition. It is designed to scare the ego back into the herd to avoid the discomfort of shaming in one form or another.

Everyone on their spirit path is going to encounter some form of shaming or another. Whether it is delivered as criticism from our spiritual peers or used by friends and families to pull you back to their point of view, this is all just another aspect of the psychological warfare that the first cognition uses against everyone to keep them in line. This is one of the saddest indictments of all against first cognition thinking under the rule of the ego - that everyone is in a constant state of battle readiness to defend themselves and their own ego in a world that demands total compliance to its rules. There can never be any real peace of mind in a paradigm based totally on conflict.

Chapter 23

"In their hostilities they shall become inventors of images and ghosts, and with those images and ghosts they shall yet fight the highest fight against one another!
Good and evil, and rich and poor, and high and low, and all names of the values: they shall be the weapons and ringing signs that life must overcome itself again and again!"

Friedrich Nietzsche - Thus Spake Zarathustra

In *A Philosophy for the Average Man* I wrote a chapter on *The Culture of Image*. It was a preliminary exposé of what is being covered in more depth in this book. The culture of image is the reflection of Nietzsche's words above. Within the first cognition, propaganda and images are used to inflame emotional passions. This use of images creates stereotypes that egos can grasp as a form of separating their particular part of the herd from other subsets of the herd. It is through creating images and ghosts and blaring them through the controlled news and media outlets that leads every human in the first cognition into conflict with every other human.

It doesn't matter the cause or the issue, whenever there is some political, religious or cultural flag to be raised as the banner to any cause, the false illusions and images create the ghosts of perception to the masses. The image of culture is nothing more than a form of perceptual sleight of hand. It is a form of illusory magic designed to misdirect egos operating in the first cognition and sow seeds of dissent to pit one group against another. Because the ego in all of us is inherently shallow and swayed by image more than substance, they are all easy to manipulate through controlled perceptions that generate emotional reactions.

Because the first cognition can only sustain its world of perceptual illusion by continuing to project more illusions, the culture of image worldwide is easily manipulable. Culture, tradition, religion and political affiliations are all projections of the self-identity of every ego. An ego can't survive on its own without the perceptual belief structures required to create its own self-image. All one needs to do to create strife is poke at any particular group ego's identifying illusion to start conflict. Poke the belief and you inflame the emotions of the individual egos whose self-identity is wrapped in that belief.

We find such manipulation through race, religions, abortion, sexual orientation, young and old, rich and poor, male against female, nation against nation and culture against culture. No matter where one turns in the realm of first cognition reality they can only find conflict. All this conflict may not necessarily lead to physical blows or wars, but the conflicts are all rooted in the self-preservation of every ego against every other ego with a differing idea or opinion. In a world governed by such selfish, self-indulgent minds, is it any wonder that humanity as a whole has not moved forward in its cognitive advancement in all of history?

Egos may profess peace, yet every one of them is in constant defense mode, ever ready for the fight that poking at their beliefs will ultimately trigger. The ego is naturally suspicious and always on guard against any such intrusions into its perceptual reality. It is ready to defend to the death, if necessary, to protect its belief structures. Human history is replete with the truth of this observation, but good luck finding any ego that is willing to admit their own responsibility in contributing to the problem. If there was ever a need for a wall of shame, the first cognition would be the poster child at the top of the list.

The knowledge of humanity has now increased so much that is has to be compartmentalized, specialized in order to be able to remotely keep track of the collection of facts that are the base of that knowledge. The tallying and recording of these facts fills libraries worldwide, yet with all this knowledge, where does one turn to find wisdom? We hear the term 'conventional wisdom' bandied about frequently. The term itself finds its origins in a 1958 book by the economist, John Kenneth Galbraith, *The Affluent Society.* But the term conventional wisdom does not represent wisdom in any form. Conventional wisdom is a misnomer predicated on the concept that certain 'facts' are widely held to be true.

As I have illustrated continuously throughout this series, the whole world of the first cognition is founded on perceptual presumptions of fact. Conventional wisdom is a term that arises when the person using the term thinks that everyone else accepts these facts as true, whether there is any truth in the perceptual presumption or not. The primary reason for resorting to conventional wisdom is to preserve the status quo where public perception is concerned.

I offer these explanations so the reader understands the basis of such terminology as another tool to reinforce first cognition perceptions. As you advance toward the second cognition it will require an advancement in your own perceptual abilities. We are all so inured to the system that we can't see how easily we use the patterns of the system in our daily lives. Operating within that system is all we know when we embark on our journey of self-discovery. At this time, many readers may feel that these are inconsequential facts, simply minor nitpicking, but this presentation is designed to alter your awareness, to make you more keenly sensitive as to how the system rules all of our minds through the most subtle of means.

Manipulating our perceptions is a manner of waging war against our consciousness. The egos who have the greed for personal power and desire world domination are fully adept at manipulating the masses through such perceptual control. This is the art of propaganda, and it has been used by egos who have the power to use it against the masses to control and sway their emotions throughout history. Many readers don't believe in mind control, or if they do, they perceive it as some kind of specialized circumstance of brainwashing like the Chinese water torture. Every ego on this planet is subject to incessant mind control from every corner of the first cognition. The most pernicious aspect of mind control is when one is completely unaware that they are being manipulated in the first place. This is called mass psychology. When one understands the emotionally reactive nature of the ego personality, projecting those reactions onto the masses is not that hard.

Cultural pressures, shame programming, guilt-laying and fear mongering of all types are each a form of mind control. Religions are particularly nasty forms of mind control, all wrapped in a presumed guise of holiness. The worst commentary is that ego-driven humans actually seek out being controlled in these fashions. They beg for external authority to guide them. It all boils down to the cult of image and how the ego personality thrives on preserving its perceptual image of itself. As you move into the second cognition, all this superficial nonsense will cease to be a required part of your consciousness, as it is a necessity only for the ego program. You will be able to fully see the counterfeit nature of all of the first cognition reality in gory detail. This will initially be very disheartening to you when you can finally see it in all its tyrannical glory, but stay the course and you will come out on the other side much more balanced and capable to deal with the lunacy that surrounds you.

I have stated that the human ego is hopelessly predictable. Those who are in power, who control the means of delivering information, are just as keenly aware of how to manipulate ego consciousness by understanding just how predictable it is. They know how to manipulate the masses through emotional reactions and they know that controlling the *public perception* is what drives their agenda for continued control.

The science fiction author Isaac Asimov created the idea of what he termed 'pyschohistory' in *The Foundation* series of science fiction books he wrote. The basic premise of the story line was tracing the history of humans into the future by using psychohistory as a measuring tool for prognosticating the future of human history by using trends of mass human behavior based on the psychology of the masses, thus the term psychohistory. Although the term was created to support a fictional story line about future happenings and presumed evolution of humanity, there is a fringe element of modern academics who think such predictions are possible. They have created *The Association for Psychohistory,* and their motto is "Putting the world on the couch."

These modern presumed psychohistorians rely on principles of Freudian psychoanalysis, history and pseudo-history as the foundation of their new pseudo-science. To date, this new schools of philosophical psychological thinking has not gained much ground in the accepted realm of academia. I am not endorsing the pseudo-science at all, but I am holding it up as another illustration of the lengths human egos will go to in order to come up with new ways to predict and control the behavior of the masses. What a wonderful world the first cognition would be if the egos of that world could accurately predict the actions of mass groups of egos for the next 500 or 1000 years!

This may seem like an arbitrary sharing of information, but the purpose is to show how *knowledgeable* and *intellectual* egos can just as easily fall into quasi-mystical desires to predict the future like any garden variety palm reader, yet wrap it in pseudo-science to justify such desires. Presumed levels of intellect are not a barrier for people falling prey to faulty systems of belief. The case study by Leon Festinger and a couple of associates that led to his presenting his Theory of Cognitive Dissonance is a prime example that deserves a closer look in light of everything that has been shared in this book.

In a synopsized form, Festinger and his two associates were able to observe a group of people for two months preceding, and one month after, believing in a doomsday prediction that ultimately failed to come to pass. For all intents and purposes, they were a small cult. Festinger started out explaining the mindset of this cult by comparing its actions to the Millerite cult that believed that the second coming of Jesus would happen on a specific date in 1843 based on the belief presented by the movement's founder William Miller. We all know that didn't happen, but the actions of the Millerites leading up to and after the fact are well documented historical events and easy to look up on the internet.

Using the Millerites as a foundational introduction to cult-type frenzy, Festinger then goes on to explain the group with which he and his associates had interface with back in the 1950's. This group had as its leader a woman who had contact with a group who called themselves the Guardians, and she received channeled messages from these Guardians, which was the basis of forming the cult. She was apparently convincing enough to draw believers into her circle and, as time went on, the Guardians told her and her followers that the world was about to be destroyed, but that their select group would be spared the cataclysm and that they would be picked up by spaceships on a certain day at a certain time. Given recent events, we can't help but see similarities to the Heaven's Gate cult.

Needless to say, the first day for the appointment with their pickup by spaceship came and went without event. The Guardians then instructed their channel that something had happened to delay the event, but that a new time would be set for a pick up. Again the assigned day and time for the pick up by the spaceship never occurred. Once again, the Guardians told the channeler that another rendezvous was assigned, which also passed without occurring.

Many of the people who bought into this doomsday cult were intelligent and many of them were affluent. Believing so deeply in the messages from the Guardians by their cult leader, many of these believers actually liquidated all their worldly goods thinking they would no longer need them because the world was coming to an end. The failure of the doomsday to actually occur left a lot of them financially destitute. It was through studying the reactions of certain cult members after the great disappointment that Festinger based his Theory of Cognitive Dissonance.

I bring up this particular case study in order to illustrate a very valid point of which I wish more people were aware. Given what I shared in previous chapters about inorganic beings manipulating human consciousness, it should be readily apparent that the alleged "Guardians" from this case study, were nothing more than a group of inorganic beings manipulating their human followers with absolutely no intent to follow up on their promises to the faithful followers of the belief. Just imagine if you can, these inorganic manipulators rolling on the floor in laughter at the package of swill they just sold this group of humans and their utter gullibility in believing such nonsense.

This case study is a prime example of the same tactic used by the presumed Galactic Federation of Light and virtually all other channeled entities that prey on gullible human consciousness. The excuses made by the Guardians about why their spaceships never showed up, and how they kept pushing out the date for the fictional pick up by those ships is the exact same ploy used over the last three decades or more by other channeled entities. The Galactic Federation of Light is one of the worst perpetrators of hanging the expectation of mother ships arriving to save the elect from the terrible world that we live in and never delivering on the goods. Just like the Guardians in Festinger's case study, the GFL continually dangles these events, and always winds up making excuses for why they didn't happen, but it will happen next time, or the next, or the next.

These occurrences are not always left to the hands of non-intellectual, gullible human beings. Phyllis Schlemmer was the primary channel for twenty years, starting in the 1970's, to an alleged group of consciousnesses known as the Council of Nine, or simply the Nine. The Nine influenced such people as Gene Roddenberry, the creator of *Star Trek*, and who named his TV series *Deep Space Nine* in honor of this group of channeled entities.

The Nine were not just channels to the stars, so to speak, they were connected with such personalities as the purported psychokinetic Uri Geller, who was associated with the Stanford Institute of Research, which was heavily involved over the years with the government research into remote viewing studies and other areas of cognitive research. Uri Geller claimed his extraordinary powers came from the Nine. The Nine seem to have had extraordinary access to high level intellectuals during the 70's, including certain governmental agencies who relied on the Nine for certain aspects of alleged intelligence gathering.

It goes beyond the scope of this book to explore the history of all of this, and any reader interested in learning about it is encouraged to do their own research into the matter. I am using Festinger's research with his associates into the Guardians cult, whatever it may have actually been called (Festinger omitted that particular piece of information from his book), to illustrate how higher level intelligences can and do work to sow disinformation and misdirection to Earth humans on a pretty regular basis. When you can see places like Stanford Institute for

Research and branches of governments being involved with these 'entities', then it denotes a serious problem with humans operating in the first cognition having no awareness of who or what they are dealing with 'out there'. We can only wonder what perceptual illusions are created to control humanity at the hands of such otherworldly influences.

Chapter 24

*"An insight has come to me. Not to the people is
Zarathustra to speak, but to companions!
Zarathustra shall not be the shepherd and dog of
a herd!"*

Friedrich Nietzsche - Thus Spake Zarathustra

I spent many years over the last two decades writing short articles and providing bits of information in varied forums and chat groups on the internet. For a long time I let myself be bothered by people not getting the message, hoping against hope to find those companions that Nietzsche wrote about. Over the many years I did this, I found a small handful of people who I consider spiritual companions who had the internal courage to advance themselves in the face of all odds. The percentage of these companions is pitiably small compared to the masses of the herd mentality who willfully refuse to entertain any ideas beyond their limited perceptual belief structures.

Just as Zarathustra had his insight that he was not to carry his messages of truth to the herd, I finally had my own insight in the same manner. You can't deliver a message to people whose ears are sealed and whose minds are utterly closed, so I decided to write this series of books for those who are open minded enough to hear the messages contained in these books. There are a lot of people who have the opportunity to advance their consciousness, but until such time as they make up their own minds and make the commitment to themselves to make this advancement, they are all marginal. They are marginal because they might make it, or they might not make it. These books are focused on two types of humans, those who still fall into the marginal column, and those who have already made the firm commitment to themselves to advance their consciousness awareness. Admittedly, I recognize that most readers of these books fall into the marginal column, but I still feel that they need the right information in their hands to be able to make an informed decision on the matter of spiritual advancement one way or the other.

This is the last book I am writing aimed at those in the marginal column. If they have not found enough information in these first four books to make an informed decision on the matter of advancing their own cognitive awareness, there is nothing else I can provide to prompt them to go there. Everything I produce from this time forward is going to be geared to providing my *companions* on this journey with many of the explanations they will need to more fully understand the second cognition.

I will make no apologies for the information in the volumes to follow this one. The information is going to be weird and hard to swallow, especially if one refuses to advance their awareness past first cognition forms of reckoning. Whether any reader after this believes the information that will be provided in future volumes or not is up to their own individual discretion and discernment. You are each totally responsible for yourselves.

I have already stated in many places that I am not standing idle waiting on others who can hold me back from my own advancement. If you want to keep up with this advancement, you are going to have to catch up, and many of you are going to have to run very hard to catch up. I am not waiting for stragglers. As you advance yourself, you would be well advised to do as little looking back at the stragglers yourself. Make your own path, move at the pace you can sustain, but always be aware of the pitfalls reported in this book and the preceding volumes. The journey is solely at your discretion. The victory of success belongs to no one but you, and it can never be taken away from you once achieved.

My father once shared a very wise piece of information with me that has guided me all my life since he shared it with me. He told me that they can take your home, your possessions, even your life, but the one thing no one can take from you is your own knowledge. I have little doubt he was speaking in reference to knowledge of the first cognition variety, but the sentiment is more relevant and true when you step into the cognitive realm of *knowing* and not simply thinking you know.

You will always have a certain amount of doubt and wondering about things. As I said, doubt as a form of healthy skepticism is not a bad thing. As these volumes progress, I have no doubt that many readers will find cause to doubt much of what will be revealed in later books. Your doubt is expected, but I also know that many of these doubts will disappear over time as you gain the experiences for yourself that allay those healthy skepticisms. I am not asking anyone to take my word for anything; your own experiences will show you whether I am yanking your chain or not. Learn to trust yourself. Learn to trust your own intuition and inner guidance and you will be guided to the answers you seek, just be aware that these answers are rarely what you expect.

Be open to what you find, but also keep that sense of healthy skepticism. Such skepticism can help one avoid the many pitfalls that navigating into the second cognition presents to us. Doubt can always be resolved when the correct inner guidance provides us with the answers to remove that doubt.

The last thought I want to leave the reader with is that along this path to moving into the second cognition, and even after you get there, you are going to make some mistakes. Don't beat yourself down when you realize you made an error in judgment. Gain wisdom from the experience and bravely move on to the next experience. Don't let your fear of making a mistake handicap your efforts to advance. You *are* going to make mistakes, *everyone* does. Accept that fact beforehand and you will be less critical of yourself when you do. To all my *companions* in this adventure, I wish you all the best and the greatest success!

Afterword

"Among my writings my Zarathustra stands by itself. With this book I have given mankind the greatest gift it has ever been given. This book, with a voice that carries over millennia, is not only the highest book that there is, the true mountain-air book — the whole fact of man lies at a tremendous distance beneath it — it is also the deepest book, born out of the innermost abundance of truth, an inexhaustible well into which no bucket descends without coming up filled with gold and goodness."

Friedrich Nietzsche - Ecce Homo, Preface § 4

Viewed strictly from the level of the first cognition consciousness, one might view Nietzsche's words as originating from arrogance, a sense of self-importance. What I hope this book has illustrated is that Nietzsche's consciousness was way ahead of his time and, having moved into the second cognition, he was equally ahead of first cognition humans of our time. In 130 years or more since he composed *Thus Spake Zarathustra*, overall human consciousness has not advanced one iota, and that is quite an indictment. By the observations and his criticisms found in *Thus Spake Zarathustra* it should be patently obvious that he was one of those who had progressed into the second cognition and felt the same desire as this author to show first cognition humans there was a better way to be found in the advancement of their own consciousness.

His contemporaries utterly failed to remotely grasp what he was trying to teach. Teachers of philosophy today still don't get the message. Nietzsche was as critical about the abuse of philosophy as I have been in the first two volumes of this series. He saw modern philosophy as having veered away from its primary function for the exploration of new ideas. Philosophy has devolved as an academic subject today even further than Nietzsche's era of the late 1800's. The criticisms he leveled against the philosophers of his time are amplified in this era. But that is what happens when first cognition egos take control of things, they can only corrupt and control, for that is the ultimate nature of the ego.

Maybe, through the presentation of the first four books in this series, we can finally gain some understanding about Nietzsche and what he was actually trying to relate to the world. The first cognition interpreters of his works over the last century or more have continued to miss what he was trying to teach humanity as a whole. It is only through advancing one's own conscious awareness that they can remotely understand what he was revealing. A re-evaluation of his works in this light is necessary.

About the Author

The author of this book is a human being who has stepped into second cognition awareness, which is open to every other human being on this planet who works to get there. The knowledge presented in this book holds more value to the reader than the identity of the author.